Kid Pix Creativity Kit

By Sherry Kinkoph

alpha books

A Division of Prentice Hall Computer Publishing
11711 North College Ave., Carmel, IN 46032 USA

To all the creative people at Broderbund, for making such an outstanding program for kids.

International Standard Book Number: 1-56761-120-6
Library of Congress Catalog Card Number: 92-75148

96   95   94   93   8   7   6   5   4   3   2   1

Interpretation of the printing code: the rightmost number of the second series of numbers is the number of the book's printing. For example, a printing code of 93-1 shows that the first printing of the book occurred in 1993.

Printed in the United States of America

Screen reproductions in this book were created by means of the program Collage Plus from Inner Media, Inc., Hollis, NH.

Trademarks

Publisher	●	Marie Butler-Knight
Associate Publisher	●	Lisa A. Bucki
Managing Editor	●	Elizabeth Keaffaber
Children's Project Manager	●	Sherry Kinkoph
Manuscript Editor	●	Audra Gable
Cover Illustrator	●	Jean Bisesi
Design & Book Production	●	Kevin Spear
Illustrations	●	Dan Ferrulli, Kevin Spear
Production Team	●	Scott Cook, Tim Cox, Mark Enochs, Phil Kitchel, Tom Loveman, Michael Nolan, Joe Ramon, Carrie Roth, Dennis Sheehan, Kelli Widdifield

Special thanks to C. Herbert Feltner for ensuring the technical accuracy of this book.

More special thanks to Lynn Noel and the students at William McKinley School #39, Indianapolis and Len Suelter at Future Kids of Indianapolis for helping to gather project ideas.

III

TABLE OF CONTENTS

V

Parents and Teachers

You've probably noticed that computers are quickly finding their way into every aspect of our lives and the lives of our children. Perhaps your child has already been exposed to the exciting world of computers, either from a computer you have at home or from a class computer found in school. If so, he or she has begun an association that will continue long into the adult years. Children love computers and are eager to learn more about what they can do. The book you are holding will help your child explore the creative side of computers.

There are many wonderful painting and graphics programs available to computer users today, but most are too "adult" to appeal to children. Broderbund, the creator of the popular Kid Pix painting program, has changed all that. Kid Pix is a colorful, noisy, imaginative painting program that challenges the creativity of children of all ages. We at Alpha Kids want to help children carry that challenge even further. The book you are holding is our way of doing that. It is a collection of exciting project ideas that will spark your child's imagination, using the Kid Pix program.

In this book, parents can find wonderful projects to share with their children. Teachers can find creative projects to use in classroom instruction. And kids can enjoy hours of fun trying them all!

Kid Pix is available for three different computer platforms: IBM-compatible, Windows, and Macintosh. The activities in this book are designed for all three of these systems. (In fact, while this book has been written specifically for use with the Kid Pix program, many of the projects can be adapted to other drawing and painting programs as well.)

We encourage you to work with your children, help them start the program, and help them assemble each craft. You may need the following tools to complete some of the projects in this book: crayons, markers or paint, scissors, tape or glue, yarn or string, hole puncher, stiff construction paper or cardboard, and a stapler.

We hope you and your children will enjoy exploring the hundreds of Kid Pix ideas we've collected. We also hope you and your children will find some ideas we didn't think about! If you do, please share them with us.

Section 1
What is Kid Pix
and What Can
I Do With It?

Hey! Welcome to my book. I'm Spike, Kid Pix artist expert, and I'm going to show you dozens of projects you can make using the Kid Pix program. You probably already have Kid Pix on your computer (that's why you bought this book), but in case you just bought the program or something, I'm going to tell you about it anyway. Kid Pix is a totally awesome computer program for really cool kids like us. With Kid Pix, you can draw, paint, write, use a bunch of rubber stamps, blow up your pictures, use coloring pages, find hidden pictures, and tons of other fun stuff. And best of all, using Kid Pix can make you a real computer whiz.

Another good thing about Kid Pix is that there are three different versions. There's a Kid Pix that works on IBM-compatible PCs (Personal computers). There's a Windows Kid Pix that works on the Windows system for PCs (Windows is a program that makes the computer easier to run). And finally, there's a Macintosh Kid Pix that works on the Macintosh computer (from Apple). So you can use one of these Kid Pix programs if you have a PC or a Macintosh—of course, you have to have the right version for your computer!

I'm going to show you how to use the Kid Pix tools, then give you some tricks and tips to follow, and hundreds of great projects to try. You'll find really easy projects, more difficult projects, and projects from kids just like you.

And just what kinds of projects am I going to show you? How about these . . .

You can use Kid Pix to create:

Postcards	Pinwheels
Holiday Ornaments	Comic Strips
Puppets	Halloween Masks
Birthday Party Kits	School Projects
Calendars	Cookbooks
and much, much more.	

I'm going to show you all sorts of cool uses for your Kid Pix program—you might not have thought of some of these projects! And best of all, I'll show you steps you need to follow to make them. (Pretty nice of me, huh? Well, we kids have got to stick together, you know.) Who knows, once you get started, you may come up with some radical stuff on your own.

You're probably ready to get started now. Turn the page and let's get going.

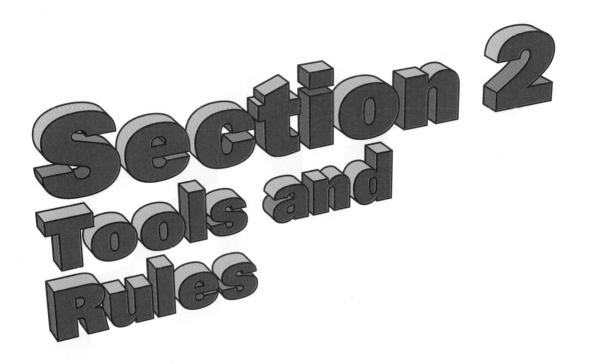

Section 2
Tools and
Rules

If you're a beginner using the Kid Pix program, you may want to read this section about how to use the program. If you already know about Kid Pix, you can go on to Section 3.

Starting Up—No Yawning!

I know that technical computer stuff can get pretty boring, but I'm about to tell you some anyway—because if you're a beginner, you really need to know it. Try not to yawn too much. I'll go fast.

For you beginners out there, let's start with how to run Kid Pix on your computer. Is it installed already? Did your mom or dad or teacher put the program onto your computer? If so, ask them where they put it and how you can make it run. They probably put it in a special computer file called a **directory**. If they did, then all you have to do is type in the word **KIDPIX** or select the Kid Pix **icon** (icon means little picture) to make it start—but ask your parents or teacher to be sure.

Steps to Start Kid Pix

Before you follow any of these steps, make sure you know what type of computer you have. If you need some help, ask your parents or teacher. (These instructions are for running the program—not installing the program.)

For IBM, IBM-compatible, or DOS computers:
- Type **C:** and press the **Enter** key.
- Type **CD\KIDPIX** and press **Enter**.
- Type **KIDPIX** and press **Enter**.

Kid Pix should start.

For Macintosh computers:
- Find the Kid Pix icon or folder in the hard disk drive window (HD).
- Double-click on the icon with your mouse pointer.
- The Kid Pix window will open up. Find the Kid Pix icon again in this next window.
- Double-click on the icon with your mouse pointer.

(If you don't know what a mouse pointer or a double-click is, see the definitions at the end of this section.)

For computers using Windows:
- Find the Kid Pix icon or folder in the Program Manager window.
- Double-click on the icon with your mouse pointer.
- The Kid Pix window will open up. Find the Kid Pix icon again in this next window.
- Double-click on the icon with your mouse pointer. (If you don't know what a mouse pointer or a double-click is, see the definitions at the end of this section.)

Screening Your Screen

Once you have Kid Pix up and running, you're ready to go. Look at your computer screen. There's a big empty square in the middle, and a strange-looking picture frame around it. The middle of the screen is your drawing area. It's like a blank piece of paper.

Hey! If you're concerned about the environment, here's something about Kid Pix for you to know. You're drawing on an *electronic* "piece of paper," so you can erase mistakes easily—and get your picture to look just the way you want it—without wasting a single piece of real paper! Yeah, Kid Pix can help save a few trees! When you've finished your picture and saved it on the computer, then you can print it out on paper.

Here's another tip: recycle your used printer paper. If you print something out and don't use it, you can put the paper back into the printer and print on the other side. This may not work for everybody—ask your parents or teacher if this is something you can do.

Wow! Now artists everywhere can help save the earth using Kid Pix!

At the top of the screen is a **menu bar**—it shows the names of the menus you can choose from: *File, Edit,* or *Goodies.* (If you have Kid Pix Companion installed on your computer, you'll see another menu called **Companion.**)

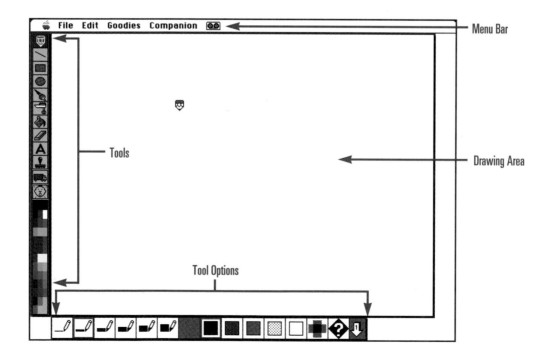

May I See A Menu?

When you start looking at computer menus, you're going to notice something right away—there's no food on these menus! (Bummer—I could really go for a hot fudge sundae right now.) Computer menus give you an easy way to make choices on the computer.

Why don't you try out a menu to see how it works? Move your **mouse pointer** up to the word **File** at the top of the screen. By the way, the mouse pointer shows how you move around on the screen. It probably looks like a little pencil on your screen when Kid Pix starts. You can draw, paint, pick out tools to use, and choose menu items using the mouse pointer. When the pointer moves out of the big empty space, it becomes an arrow. (I guess that's why they call it a **pointer**, huh? I'm such a genius!)

When you've moved the pointer to the word **File**, press the mouse button and hold it down. (IBM and Windows users should always remember to use the left mouse button.) A menu pops up on your screen. As soon as you let go of your mouse button, it disappears again. (Windows program users: you don't have to worry about this on your program. When you select a menu with your mouse, it stays up on your screen without having to hold the mouse button down. Aren't you lucky?) To see what's on the menu, you have to keep holding the mouse button down. When you want to choose something from the menu, move the mouse pointer down the menu, *while* you're still holding the mouse button, till you find the right item. Each item you point to suddenly gets a black box around it. That's called **highlighting**.

This is pretty tricky stuff, but with a little practice, you'll get the hang of it.

Practice Makes Perfect

Just to practice, let's choose **Quit** from the menu. Move your mouse to the very bottom of the menu where it says "Quit." (Windows users, your menu will say "Exit".) There's a picture of a little hand waving next to the word Quit. Now let go of the mouse button. What happened?

The program stopped, and you're back at the very beginning again. Don't worry—you need some practice starting Kid Pix anyway.

So that's how you choose something from the menu. Now start Kid Pix back up again (follow the instructions in the box at the beginning of this section if you need help).

Keyboard Shortcuts

Lots of computer programs have quicker ways to use menus without ever touching the mouse. Instead of pulling down menus, you type a combination of keys on the keyboard to select menu items. These are called **keyboard shortcuts**. Kid Pix has keyboard shortcuts too. But you have to memorize which keys to type and which menu they choose from. It's best to stick to using the mouse and menus for now.

Did you just yawn? Well cut it out. I'm almost through telling you about this technical stuff. You want to know how to use the program, don't you? Chill out. You'll thank me later.

Cool Tools

When you have Kid Pix back on your computer screen, look at the left side of the screen. That's where all your **tools** are. Tools are things you use to draw, paint, make boxes or circles, and more. At the bottom of your screen is where the **tool options** are (options are extra things you can do with the tools). This is called the **tool option bar**. The best way to learn what the tools do is to try them yourself.

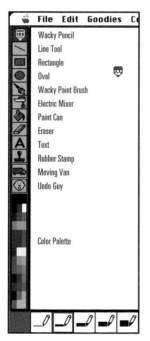

To choose a tool, move the mouse pointer over to the one you want. **Click** the mouse button. (Clicking is pressing or tapping the mouse button once—do it twice in a row and it's called **double-clicking**.) Now you've chosen a tool. Move the mouse pointer out into the drawing area. Sometimes the pointer will even become the shape of the tool you picked, like a pencil or paint brush. Pretty cool, huh?

When you pick a tool, like the Wacky Pencil, that has lots of options, you'll see this icon at the end of the tool option bar. Use the mouse pointer to click on this and the tool options will change. Now you have more options to choose from. What a variety!

To use most tools, you have to hold down the mouse button and move the mouse all at the same time. This takes some coordination. If your mom made you take piano lessons (like mine did), this might be easier for you. It's kind of like walking and chewing gum at the same time. If you can do that, you can do this. Now, if you're *really* into a challenge, try this: hold the mouse button down, move the mouse, **AND** chew gum all at the same time. That's coordination! (Just don't get any gum on the computer or you'll get yelled at.)

The Rules

Well, I know you don't want to hear about rules, but . . . I do need to warn you about a couple of things. It's my job, since this is my book. Besides, your computer will thank me for it.

1. Never just shut off your computer while you are using Kid Pix. Use the File menu to quit.

2. You are only able to draw inside the drawing area on your screen. You can't make your page any bigger. You'll have to remember this when you print something out on your printer, too.

3. Never bring food or drinks near your computer. If you spill something, it could get inside and ruin your computer forever. Pretty serious stuff!

4. If you have any problems at all, get a grown-up to help you as soon as possible. I know they're not always as cool as we are, but they're good at helping out when you're in trouble, like when your computer is smoking or something.

Okay, so play with these tools and learn these rules and you'll be a Kid Pix artist in no time. Read the next section to find out about neat tricks to try.

WORDS TO THE WISE

click: one quick press or tap of the mouse button.

directory: a special computer file, like a folder, where you can save and keep your programs and stuff.

double-click: two quick presses or taps of the mouse button.

highlighting: when a menu item gets a black box around it.

icon: a little picture that stands for something. For example, stands for Kid Pix.

menu: a list of choices—an easy way to make choices on the computer.

menu bar: the long, skinny box at the very top of your screen that shows the different menu names.

mouse pointer: a point on the computer screen that moves when you move the mouse around.

tool options: extra things your tools can do.

tools: things you use to draw, paint, make boxes or circles, and more.

Tool Definitions

(There's a quick sheet you can tear out at the back of this book that has all the tool definitions on it too!)

Wacky Pencil—draws just like a real pencil. You can even choose how thick your pencil is by using the tool options. You can pick a square or a circle pencil. The pencil can also draw in a pattern, or a rainbow of colors. You can't do these things with a real pencil!

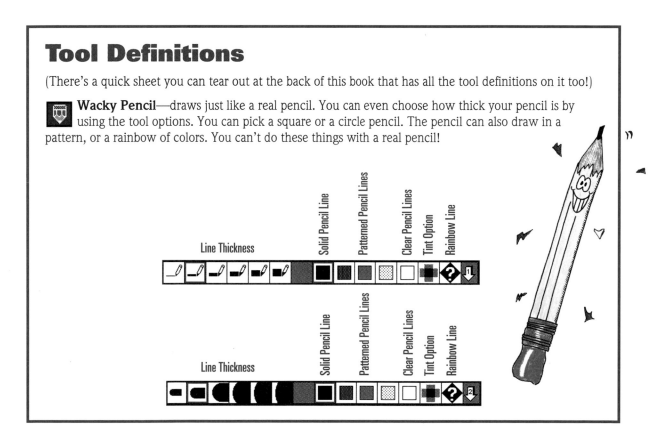

Tool Definitions (continued)

Line Tool—draws straight lines. You can choose different thicknesses and patterns to use. You'll never need a ruler again.

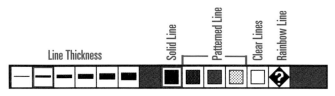

Rectangle—draws boxes shaped like rectangles or squares. The option bar lets you pick empty boxes, solid boxes, or patterned boxes.

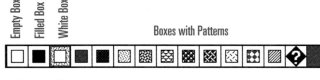

Oval—this tool works the same way as the rectangle tool, except it draws circles and ovals instead.

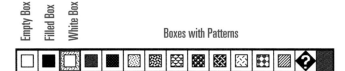

Wacky Brush—acts like a paintbrush. You can choose different colors to paint with from the color palette. (A real palette is a thin board or tablet that artists use to mix their colors on. A computer palette lets you choose from different colors or shades.) The Wacky Brush has lots of tool options. You'll want to try each one to see what it does.

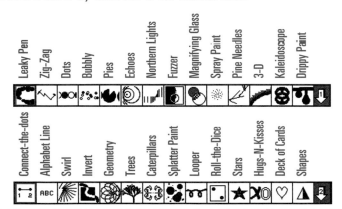

Electric Mixer—scrambles up your picture in a variety of ways. This is another tool that you'll want to see what each option does. You can use this tool to make some really funky pictures.

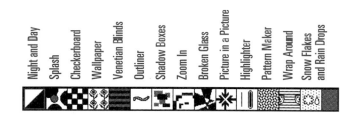

Night and Day · Splash · Checkerboard · Wallpaper · Venetian Blinds · Outliner · Shadow Boxes · Zoom In · Broken Glass · Picture in a Picture · Highlighter · Pattern Maker · Wrap Around · Snow Flakes and Rain Drops

Paint Can—I also call this a Paint Bucket, because that's what it looks like to me. This tool fills up your space with whatever color or pattern you pick. Wherever you point the little drop of paint pouring out of the bucket, that's where your space will fill up with color or pattern.

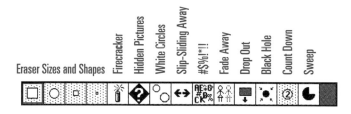

Solid Paint · Patterns · Rainbow Effect

Eraser—this tool lets you erase parts of your picture or the whole thing. Using the tool options, you can pick different ways to clear your screen. There's even a firecracker stick for "blowing up" your picture.

Eraser Sizes and Shapes · Firecracker · Hidden Pictures · White Circles · Slip-Sliding Away · #$%!*!! · Fade Away · Drop Out · Black Hole · Count Down · Sweep

Alphabet Tool—lets you stamp letters of the alphabet all over your drawing. Also includes numbers!

A B C D E F G H I J K L M N ↓

Rubber Stamp—lets you use little pictures that look like rubber stamps. You can stamp them wherever you want on your drawing. There are lots to choose from and they vary from IBM version to Mac version.

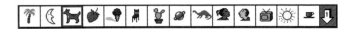

Moving Van—lets you move pieces of your picture from one spot to another on your screen. It's kind of like using a pair a scissors to cut out a piece and stick it somewhere else.

The Undo Guy—this is great! It lets you undo whatever you just did. So if you made a mistake, this will take it away.

Color Palette—if you've got a color monitor, you'll see lots of different colors you can use with your tools. If you've got a monochrome (black and white) monitor, you'll see shades of gray. If you have a color printer, you can even print out your projects in colors. If you don't, you'll have to color them in after you've printed them.

Windows Palette   Mac Palette

Menu Madness

Here's a little help explaining the Kid Pix menus.

FILE MENU—this is where you can save your pictures, make new files, print, and quit. (Files are like little folders where you save your Kid Pix work.)

New—this opens up a new drawing screen for you. It's like getting out a new piece of paper to work on.

Open—this lets you open up pictures you've already made—if you saved them, that is.

Close—this puts your drawing screen away. (This menu item isn't on the IBM version.)

Save—this will save your picture and ask you to name it. Name it something to help you remember what it is. You'll need to remember to save pictures you've made if you want to keep them to see, or to work on again. Don't save the ones you don't like, though. Every time you save something, it takes up room in the computer's memory.

Save As—this saves your picture automatically, and asks you to name it.

Page Set-Up—using this, you can tell the printer how you want to print your picture: sideways or up and down. Be sure to ask your parents or a teacher for some help when you print the first time. Everyone has different types of printers. (This menu item is not available on the IBM version of the program.)

Print—this tells your computer to print your work.

Quit—gee, can you figure out what this does? This stops the Kid Pix program.

EDIT MENU—you can fix up things on your picture with this menu, or make copies, or even erase.

Undo—this works the same way as the Undo Guy tool. It undoes whatever you did last.

Cut—this is like having a pair of scissors: you can cut out parts of your work. Use this with the Moving Van tool.

Copy—lets you copy parts of your work. Use this with the Moving Van tool, too.

Paste—this will let you put whatever you cut or copied onto your drawing, wherever you want. You have to use the mouse to help you. When the pasted item is where you want it, click your mouse button. You can even paste parts from other pictures you saved. Cool!

Clear—kind of like the eraser, but you use it with the Moving Van tool to clear parts of your picture.

GOODIES MENU—full of stuff to do to your Kid Pix program.

Small Kids Mode—lets you fix the Kid Pix screen so your little brother or sister can't accidentally mess up your files and stuff. It takes the menu bar off the top of the screen. So next time your kid sister or brother wants to play with Kid Pix, just turn this menu item on—then they can't goof up all your hard work. Good thing they invented this!

Mac Goodies Menu

17

Menu Madness (continued)

Edit Stamp—this is great! Whatever stamp your Rubber Stamp tool is showing in the options bar, you can use this to change how it looks. You can even create your own brand new stamps! Look for the Edit Stamp box on page 19 that tells you how to use it.

Alphabet Text—if you're using the Wacky Paintbrush tool's **ABC** option, this item lets you type in new letters, numbers, or symbols to use. When you choose this from the menu, a box will pop up on your screen—you can type in whatever you want, and save it by clicking on **OK**. Now the new letters you typed and saved will appear when you use the Wacky Paintbrush ABC tool.

Four of the next five menu items are used if your computer system has sound. If your computer doesn't have sound, you don't have to worry about these menu items, they won't work for you. Ask your parents or a teacher to find out if you can have sound on your computer.

Turn Tool Sounds Off—getting tired of all the noise Kid Pix makes? Pick this item off the menu to turn every noise off. (The Mac version of Kid Pix just says **Tool Sounds** for this menu item.)

Switch To Spanish—this is a great menu tool. It lets you change the language of the Kid Pix program to Spanish.

Pick A Song—use this to choose a song to go with your picture. Experiment and see what happens. (The Mac version doesn't have this function.)

Record Sound—you can choose this from the menu to record your own sounds to go with your pictures. It's kind of like having a tape recorder. You'll want some help with this the first time you use it, and your computer must have a microphone. (The IBM version doesn't have this function.)

Play Sound—lets you play back what you recorded using the Record Sound function. (Sorry—not on the IBM version.)

Edit Stamp

To change or create your own stamps, first choose the Rubber Stamp tool. Now pick which stamp you want to edit from the bottom of the screen (*edit* means to fix up). Move your mouse pointer to the **Goodies** menu and choose **Edit Stamp**.

You'll see a big picture of the stamp you chose in a little drawing screen. Try out the editing tools to see what they do. Don't worry about ruining a stamp—the program always keeps a copy, and you can restore it at any time.

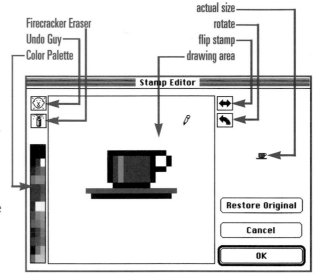

Let's say you wanted to change the Cup stamp to look like it has steam coming out of it, like a cup of hot cocoa. Use the pencil tool to draw lines coming out of the cup. (If you make a mistake, point to the Undo Guy and click.) When you've drawn everything the way you want it, choose **OK**. If you want to design your own stamp, use the dynamite stick to clear the drawing screen, and then you can start with a clean drawing area.

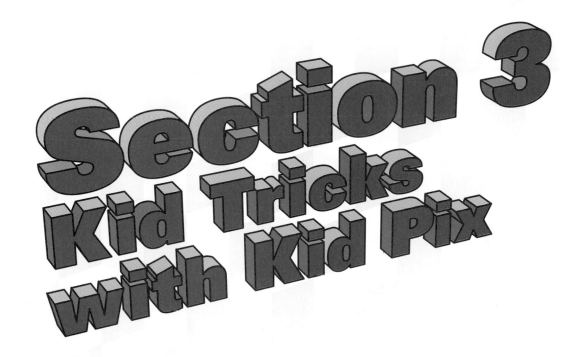

Section 3
Kid Tricks
with Kid Pix

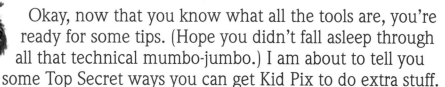

Okay, now that you know what all the tools are, you're ready for some tips. (Hope you didn't fall asleep through all that technical mumbo-jumbo.) I am about to tell you some Top Secret ways you can get Kid Pix to do extra stuff. You must promise not to tell anyone. They'll think you're a kid genius for knowing all this stuff. Of course, maybe you figured all this out on your own—then you really *are* a genius—or you learned how to hit all the lucky buttons!

I Need a Straight Line

If you're having trouble drawing a straight line with the Line tool, here's a tip for you. While you're using the Line tool, hold down the **Shift** key on your keyboard. If you're drawing a horizontal line (left to right), this will keep it straight. If you're drawing a vertical line (up and down), holding down the **Shift** key will keep it straight. If you're drawing a line at a 45-degree angle (slanted), this trick will make it nice and straight without all those little jagged edges.

Tips for Ovals and Rectangles

If you've ever used the tools that make ovals and circles —or rectangles and squares—you may have noticed the third tool option that lets you draw a box or circle filled in with white, and puts a line all around the edge. Sometimes you might not want this border.

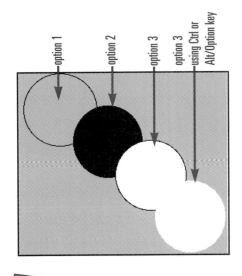

option 1
option 2
option 3
option 3 using Ctrl or Alt/Option key

No problem. Just hold down the **Ctrl** key (IBM and Windows users) or the **Alt/Option** key (Mac users) while you're drawing the shape. This will draw the shape without the border.

Are you having trouble drawing perfect circles or squares? Hold down the **Shift** key while drawing the shape—it'll come out perfect.

 One more funky thing about ovals and rectangles. If you hold down the **Ctrl** key (IBM and Windows users) or the **Alt/Option** key (Mac users) and use the tool option, the oval or rectangle will fill up with shades of gray when you finish drawing the shape.

Wacky Paint Brush Tips

Many of the Paint Brush tool options do strange things when you use the tool and hold down the **Ctrl** key (IBM and Windows users) or **Alt/Option** key (Mac users). Look on your computer's keyboard to find these keys, and remember where they are.

I'm going to tell you all about the tricks you can do with the Wacky Paint Brush, but first you have to remember this very important thing: IBM and Windows users must use the **Ctrl** key and Mac users must use the **Alt/Option** key to make all of this stuff work. Also, some of these tricks don't work on certain systems, but I'll tell you when they don't. Okay, there are a lot of these Paint Brush tips, so hang in there.

TRICKS OF THE TRADE

If you're a Mac user, holding down the **Alt/Option** key will change the Leaky Pen tool as it draws. It changes to look like a ripple of water in a puddle—circles inside of circles. Try it!

The Zig Zag tool draws bigger zig zags when you hold down the **Ctrl** key or **Alt/Option** key.

The Dots tool draws more dots when you hold down the **Ctrl** key or the **Alt/Option** key.

If you're an IBM or Windows user, hold down the **Ctrl** key while using the Bubbly tool, and your bubbles will become a rainbow of colors.

The Pies tool becomes outlines when you hold down the **Ctrl** key or **Alt/Option** key.

The Echoes tool becomes solid, filled-in echoes when you hold down the **Ctrl** key or the **Alt/Option** key.

The Fuzzer tool makes bigger fuzzy areas when you hold down the **Ctrl** key or the **Alt/Option** key.

The Spray Paint tool will make a square instead of a circle effect when you hold down the **Ctrl** or **Alt/Option** key.

The Magnifying Glass tool will magnify even larger when you press **Ctrl** or **Alt/Option**.

The Pine Needles tool makes thicker pine needles when you hold down the **Ctrl** or **Alt/Option** key.

For IBM and Windows users, hold down the **Ctrl** key while using the 3-D tool, and you'll get a rainbow.

The Kaleidoscope works in two different ways—one way for IBM and Windows users, and another for Mac users. When IBM and Windows users hold down the **Ctrl** key, the Kaleidoscope makes thicker lines. When Mac users hold down the **Alt/Option** key, the Kaleidoscope makes funny black lines.

IBM

MAC

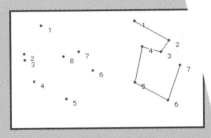

The Connect-the-Dots tool is tricky. When you use the tool, dots are numbered as you move the mouse while holding down the mouse button, and lines are drawn between the numbered dots. When you stop using the tool, the lines between the dots go away. If you want to keep the lines, press the **Ctrl** or **Alt/Option** key while you draw with the tool. If you want to draw your dots farther apart, just click each dot in place—one at a time by pressing the mouse button each time you get to a place where you want a dot to appear. They'll still come out numbered dots.

IBM and Windows users can get a rainbow effect out of the Swirl tool by holding down the **Ctrl** key. Mac users can't get this effect—nothing happens.

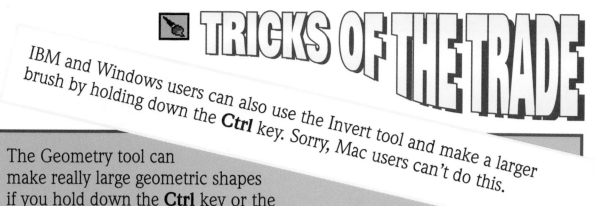

TRICKS OF THE TRADE

IBM and Windows users can also use the Invert tool and make a larger brush by holding down the **Ctrl** key. Sorry, Mac users can't do this.

The Geometry tool can make really large geometric shapes if you hold down the **Ctrl** key or the **Alt/Option** key.

The Splatter Paint tool turns into splatter triangles if you hold down the **Ctrl** or **Alt/Option** key.

You can make bigger trees with the Tree tool if you hold down the **Ctrl** key or the **Alt/Option** key.

For IBM and Windows users, hold down the **Ctrl** key with the Looper tool and get a rainbow loop.

Is Your Mixer Plugged In?

A few of the Electric Mixer tools change a little also when you press the **Ctrl** key or the **Alt/Option** key and use them. I'm not going to tell you which ones. You can try them on your own and be surprised.

Freeze Your Firecracker

Here's a good tip to try when you're using the Firecracker eraser tool. You can freeze the exploding effect when you press the **Ctrl** key (IBM, Windows users) or the **Alt/Option** key (Mac users). You can make some very interesting pictures using this trick. Just choose the Firecracker eraser tool, put your mouse pointer on the screen where you want the explosion to start. As your picture explodes, you can freeze it at any time using the **Ctrl** or **Alt/Option** key. Try it several times on the same picture to make some really cool designs.

You can also freeze the Drop Out eraser tool by using the same trick.

Can You Type with This Thing?

Are you getting tired of stamping letters all over your picture when you want to spell out a word or sentence? Well, have I got a trick for you. You can turn your Kid Pix into a word processor! (Word processing means working with words.) All you have to do is hold down the **Ctrl** key or the **Alt/Option** key as you select the Text Tool. Notice what happens in the tool option bar at the bottom.

Now you have several different styles of letters to choose from. Pick one you want to try, place your pointer where you want the words to appear on your

screen and click the button. Now you can start typing on the keyboard, and the letters will appear on your screen. Cool!

Sizeable Stamps

The Rubber Stamp tool is a lot of fun to use. But I've got a few tricks you might like to try. You can make your stamps bigger. You can double the size of the rubber stamp if you hold down the **Ctrl** key (IBM, Windows users) or **Alt/Option** key (Mac users) while you stamp the picture. IBM and Windows users can also triple the size of the stamps by holding down the **Ctrl** key and the **Shift** key at the same time. Mac users can do this by just holding down the **Shift** key while stamping the picture. Mac users can make their stamps even bigger by holding down the **Alt/Option** key and the **Shift** key at the same time.

Mac Stamps

Get a Move On It!

Here's a tip for using the Moving Van. You can use the Magnet tool and the **Ctrl** key (IBM, Windows) or the **Alt/Option** key (Mac) to copy sections of your picture. Let's say you've drawn a really nice picture of a cheeseburger—gee, I could really go for one of those right now—and you want to copy it and put another cheeseburger

28

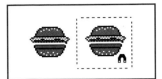

right next to the first one. Use the Magnet to surround your burger with a blinking box. (You've got to hold down the mouse button to do this.) Next, hold down the **Ctrl** or **Alt/Option** key while you move your "magnetized" section to wherever you want to put the copy. (To move the section, hold down your mouse button and move the mouse.) Let go of the mouse button and—Voilà!—your burger has doubled! It's a double cheeseburger! Now how about some fries with that?

Printing Tips

Depending on what kind of computer system you have (and what kind of printer is hooked up to it), your printing will vary. Some printers will let you print a drawing that takes up the whole piece of paper. Others just print a picture the size of your Kid Pix screen. Because of this, the size of your projects may differ from what I am going to show you.

But being the clever kid you are, you can do some pretty creative things to work around this. For example, the first project I'm going to show you how to make is Gift Wrap. (Yes—you can use Kid Pix to design your own gift wrap patterns!) If your printer prints a small picture of your gift wrap—and it's too small to wrap a gift with—just print out several copies of the gift wrap pattern. Then cut them out and tape them together to make a bigger sheet.

Steps to making bigger gift wrap sheets

You may have to use this artistic technique for several projects. But be creative—we kids can be very talented, you know.

That's Enough

All right. That's all the tricks I know. I hope you have fun trying them. I think you're ready for a project by now.

In the rest of this book, you'll find projects for all sorts of occasions. You'll find things you can make for parents, teachers, brothers and sisters, friends, your dog—and yourself. The important thing is to have fun, be creative, and learn what a cool computer drawing program Kid Pix is. You don't have to be an artist to use Kid Pix. In fact, you don't even have to be a kid to use Kid Pix. (But don't tell grown-ups that, or they'll hog the computer all day long.)

Section 4
Easy Projects

SWIFT GIFT WRAP

Materials needed:
crayons/markers/paint,
tape, scissors
Optional: glitter, bows

Now you can design your own gift wrap for any occasion using Kid Pix. You can make gift wrap for birthdays, holidays, weddings, and more. You can even personalize your gift wrap with names. This swift gift wrap idea can really make your gift-giving special. (You do want everyone to think they're special, don't you?)

STEP 1 Decide on the style and theme of the gift wrap. Is it for a birthday? Christmas? Do you want to design it yourself or use the Kid Pix rubber stamps? What tools are you going to use? Figure all that out, then make your design.

STEP 2 Next, fill the drawing screen with your gift wrap pattern. You don't need to color it yet, because you're going to print it out and then color it (unless you have a color printer). Don't forget to save your design if you want to use it again!

STEP 3 Print out your gift wrap design. (Remember to pull down the File menu and choose **Print**.) Color in your design using crayons, markers, or paint. You may even want to glue on glitter, bows, funny buttons, whatever you can think of.

TIP: If you're wrapping larger presents, you'll need to print out several copies of your gift wrap pattern and tape them together to form a big sheet of wrapping paper.

STEP 4 Wrap your gift! That's all there is to it!

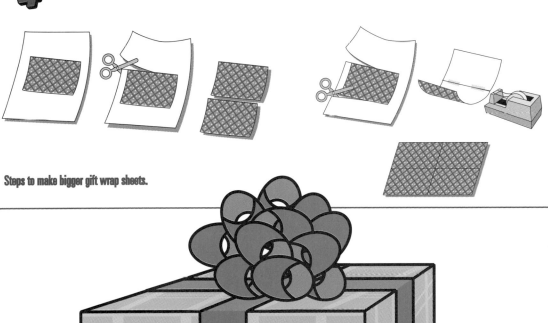

Steps to make bigger gift wrap sheets.

PERSONAL POSTCARDS

Materials needed:
crayons/markers/paint,
glue, scissors, thin cardboard

You don't have to go on a vacation to send postcards. You can create your own to send to friends and relatives. Just use your imagination to draw pictures of places in your own town, or neighborhood. Or how about a drawing of you and your house? Or maybe your dog, cat, or goldfish? You can make all sorts of fun postcards to send.

Dear Bobbie,
I got a
new Computr
program called
Kid Pix.
It's great!

—Spike

Bob Maroony
101 North St.
Kroonie, OR
xxxxx

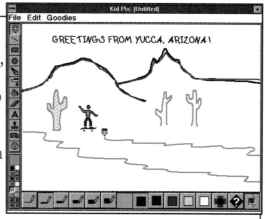

STEP 1 Decide what you want to draw on your postcard. A neighborhood scene, family members, your backyard? Use Kid Pix to create your picture. Remember to keep your drawing small enough to be a postcard. Postcards usually measure 3-1/2 inches by 5-1/2 inches or 4 inches by 6-1/4 inches. (It may take a little experimenting to get the size right when you print your postcard.)

STEP 2 Print out your postcard. Color it with crayons, markers, or paint and cut it out.

STEP 3 Paste or glue your postcard to a thin piece of cardboard. (Like the stiff cardboard found in back of pads of paper, or gift boxes.)

Dear Bob,
My mom says you can come out to visit us on vacation. Isn't that great?
Now I can show you my skateboard collection. There's a great hill down the street where we can try them all out. But you'd better bring some knee pads.

See ya soon!

Your buddy, Spike

Bob Splob
90211 West Hobb Street
Grob, Wisconsin
71298

Stamp

POSTCARD BY SPIKE

STEP 4 Go back to your Kid Pix program and create the other side of the postcard. Use the word processor trick (from Section 3 in this book) to type a message using Kid Pix. Your postcard message should be on the left side. The name and address of the person you're sending it to should be on the right side. Don't forget to leave room for a stamp in the upper right corner!

STEP 5 Print out the message side of your postcard. Sign your name, and make sure you put the name and address of the person you are sending the postcard to.

STEP 6 Paste or glue the message side of the postcard to the back of the postcard picture you made in Step 3. Now you can mail your postcard to a friend or relative. (Don't forget to put a postage stamp on it!)

More ideas: You can make postcards for all occasions. Here are some other postcard ideas . . . holidays, birthdays, imaginary trips, thank you's, party invitations. Get creative and think of some more!

Visit the Southwest

AWESOME AWARDS

Materials needed:
crayons/markers/paint, scissors
Optional: glue and glitter

You can design your own award certificates for teachers or parents. For example, impress your teacher and make him or her a Teacher of the Year certificate. Make an official Father's Day or Mother's Day award. Make a gift certificate for helping Mom or Dad with household chores, car washing, or yard work.

STEP 1 Choose what kind of award certificate you are going to make. Write down what you would like it to say.

STEP 2 Create the certificate using the Kid Pix program. You can make a fancy border by making huge squares on your Kid Pix screen, add an official-looking seal, and type up the words using the Kid Pix letters (see the word processing trick in Section 3 of this book).

STEP 3 Print out your certificate.

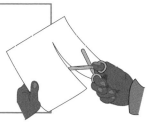 **STEP 4** Color in your certificate with crayons, markers, or paint. You can also glue on glitter or other stuff to make it look interesting.

 STEP 5 If you need to, cut out your certificate and trim it nicely. Now you've got a great award to give!

More ideas: You can also make great certificates for friends and relatives, prize certificates for games, and club awards. Use your imagination!

Tip: You can copy Kid Pix pictures and art into other graphics and drawing programs. You can also copy art from other graphics programs into Kid Pix. Using the Moving Van tool, the Copy and Paste commands from the Edit menu, and the clipboard to move around your files. Have a parent or teacher help you the first time.

To the Best Mom in the World

Thanks for doing all the cooking, cleaning, car-pooling, lunch-making, and homework-helping! You're the best Mom ever!

Love, Sally

PEACHY PINWHEEL

Materials needed:
crayons/markers/paint, scissors,
wooden stick or straw, tack, glue

Create a custom-designed pinwheel that really works.
Pinwheels make great toys, especially for younger
sisters or brothers.

STEP 1 Decide what kind of design you
would like to make for your
pinwheel. Use the Kid Pix program to
make your pinwheel pattern on the screen. But
here's an important thing to remember: your
pinwheel needs to be a perfect square! (You can
draw a perfect square with Kid Pix using the trick
in section 3—hold down the **Ctrl** key (IBM,
Windows users) or **Alt/Option** key (Mac users)
while using
the Rectangle
tool. Or you
can just cut
out your
printed
picture into a
perfect
square.)

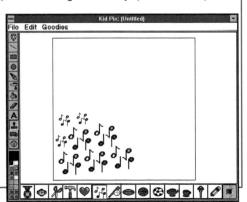

STEP 2 Print
out your
pinwheel, and color it
using crayons, markers, or
paint.

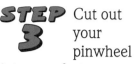 **STEP 3** Cut out your pinwheel into a perfect square (if it's not already a perfect square).

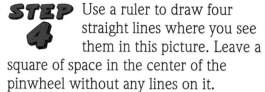 **STEP 4** Use a ruler to draw four straight lines where you see them in this picture. Leave a square of space in the center of the pinwheel without any lines on it.

STEP 5 Use scissors to cut the four straight lines.

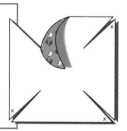

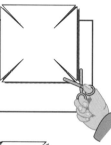

STEP 6 Turn your pinwheel over so the colored side is down. Now glue, staple or tape one corner of each side of the pinwheel to the center of the pinwheel. Just so you know what I'm talking about, I've marked the correct corners with X's. Follow this picture.

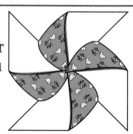

STEP 7 Poke a hole in the center of the pinwheel, through all four folded-down and glued corners. Tack your pinwheel center to a stick or straw with a thumbtack or a small nail. (If you use a straw, you may have to glue the thumbtack in.) It's important to leave some extra space on the tack or nail so the pinwheel can spin. If you tack it on too tightly, it won't spin at all.

Now you can wave your pinwheel in the air and make it spin!

FLASHY FLASH CARDS

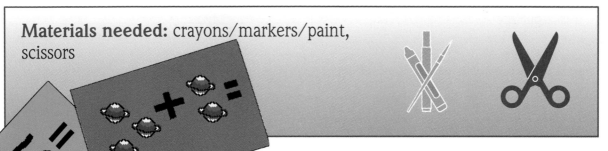

Materials needed: crayons/markers/paint, scissors

Make your own flash cards to help you with math or reading, or make some for your little brother or sister.

STEP 1 Choose what kind of flash card you are going to make. Addition? Subtraction? Multiplication? Division? Spelling? Write down the math problems or spelling words you are going to make. If you decide to make cards with answers on them, make sure they're the correct answers. You wouldn't want to memorize the wrong answers to your multiplication tables, would you?

STEP 2 Use Kid Pix to create each flash card. You can make big flash cards, little flash cards, or any size in-between. I made some addition flash cards for my little brother to practice on. I used the Kid Pix stamps to make things for him to count.

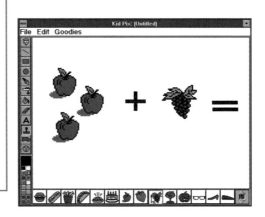

STEP 3 Print out each flash card, and color it in using crayons, markers, or paint.

Now you can help your friends, family, or yourself memorize letters, words, and numbers.

STEP 4 Cut out your flash cards. If you want, you can glue or paste them to thicker pieces of cardboard.

RAIN

Name these musical instruments

More ideas: Use flash cards to help you with your spelling list, word definitions, and more. Help your little brother or sister learn shapes, colors, animals, alphabet letters, and numbers!

5 ÷

RAIN

41

FLASH CARD VARIATIONS

Teacher, Lynn Noel, and the kids at William McKinley Elementary School #39 in Indianapolis came up with some great projects for flash cards. Here are their ideas:

MAKE NUMBER PUZZLE FLASH CARDS

STEP 1 Use the Line tool to divide your Kid Pix screen in half—straight down the middle.

STEP 2 Stamp or write (using the Pencil tool) a number from 1 to 10 on one side of the flash card.

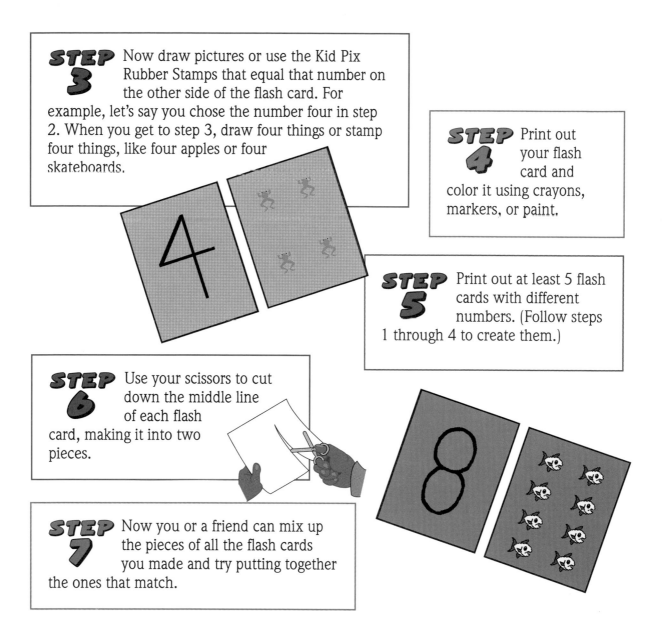

STEP 3 Now draw pictures or use the Kid Pix Rubber Stamps that equal that number on the other side of the flash card. For example, let's say you chose the number four in step 2. When you get to step 3, draw four things or stamp four things, like four apples or four skateboards.

STEP 4 Print out your flash card and color it using crayons, markers, or paint.

STEP 5 Print out at least 5 flash cards with different numbers. (Follow steps 1 through 4 to create them.)

STEP 6 Use your scissors to cut down the middle line of each flash card, making it into two pieces.

STEP 7 Now you or a friend can mix up the pieces of all the flash cards you made and try putting together the ones that match.

Special thanks to 2nd graders Roy Millbrooks and Gladys Weger for sending me that flash card puzzle idea.

FLASH CARD VARIATIONS

BEGINNING SOUNDS PUZZLE

STEP 1 Use the Line tool to divide your Kid Pix screen in half—straight down the middle.

STEP 2 On one side of the screen, draw a letter for the beginning sound of a word, like a big D or H.

STEP 3 On the other side of the screen, draw some pictures of things that begin with that sound. If you used a D in step 2, you could draw a dog or dollar in step 3.

STEP 4 Print out your flash card and color it.

STEP 5 Print out at least 5 flash cards with different letters and pictures. (Follow steps 1 through 4 to create them.)

STEP 6 Use your scissors to cut down the middle line of each flash card making it into two pieces.

STEP 7 Now you or a friend can mix up the pieces of all the flash cards you made and try putting together the ones that match.

Special thanks to 6th grader Jason Noel for that idea.

45

FLASH CARD VARIATIONS

RHYMING PUZZLES

STEP 1 Use the Line tool to divide your Kid Pix screen in half—straight down the middle.

 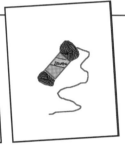

STEP 2 On each side of the screen, draw pictures of things that rhyme. For example, on one side you could draw a hat. On the other side, you could draw a cat. Be sure to write the word out too. You can use your Kid Pix Alphabet stamps to help you.

STEP 3 Print out your flash card and color it.

STEP 4 Print out at least 5 flash cards with different rhyming words and pictures. (Follow steps 1 through 3 to create them.)

STEP 5 Use your scissors to cut down the middle line of each flash card making it into two pieces.

STEP 6 Now you or a friend can mix up the pieces of all the flash cards you made and try putting together the ones that match.

Special thanks to 2nd graders Jason Arbuckle, Michelle Hendrickson, Malvin Harlin, Bridgette Sanders, and Nefetia Ogletree for sending me these ideas.

Section 5
Holiday Projects

VALENTINES

Why give boring old store-bought valentines when you can make your own designer valentines to give to friends and loved ones? With Kid Pix, card-making is easy!

STEP 1 Well, you can figure out how to make all sorts of cards using Kid Pix, but I'm going to show you how to make some unusual ones. Have you ever made cut-out cards before? Cut-out cards have parts of the card cut out to reveal the inside of the card. The cut-out card I'm going to show you has a heart peeking up over the top of the card. (I know it's pretty mushy, but it's for my mom. Really.)

The first thing you do is design your card using Kid Pix. Notice how I drew a heart on the right side of the card? That's going to be the front of the card. The left side of the picture is going to be the back of the card. (You can leave the inside blank to write your name in it.)

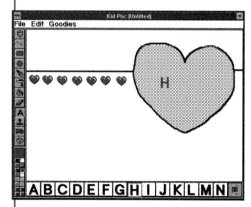

STEP 2 Print out your valentine, and color it using crayons, markers, or paint. You may even want to glue on glitter or sequins to make it sparkle.

STEP 3 Use scissors to cut the top of the card so the heart peeks out over the top.

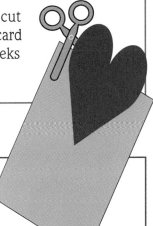

STEP 4 Fold your card, with the picture side on the outside. Now find an envelope to fit it in, and you're ready to give your heart away! (At least your mom will like it.)

Mom!

Tip: If you're really clever, you can print up the inside part of the card with a Valentine's message, and glue the two sides of the card together. Or you can print out the outer part of the card, flip it over, and run the same piece of paper through the printer again to print up an inside message. This is very tricky. Get a parent or teacher to help you.

TEENY TINY EASTER BASKET

Materials needed:
crayons/markers/
paint, scissors,
glue, tape
Optional: staples
and stapler

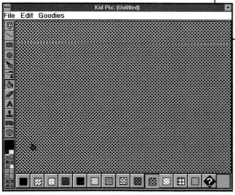

Why should the Easter Bunny have all the fun? Use Kid Pix to create a small Easter basket to decorate or give as a gift!

STEP 1 Create your basket pattern. I used the woven-looking pattern in the Paint Bucket tool option, and filled the whole screen with it. (If your screen prints bigger than the Kid Pix drawing screen, create a rectangle the size of the drawing screen, and fill it with the pattern.)

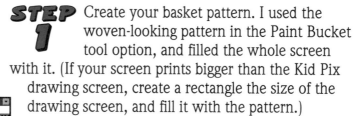

STEP 2 Print out your drawing and color it in using crayons, markers or paint. Easter colors would be good (light blue, light yellow, light green, pink).

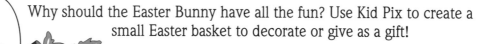

50

STEP 3 Cut out the rectangle shape of the basket. Now you have to be careful: cut one-inch-long straight lines at each corner. Follow this picture.

STEP 4 Use tape, staples or glue and fold the corners in, just the way this picture shows.

STEP 5 Go back to the Kid Pix program and make a long, narrow rectangle. Fill it in with the same pattern you used on the basket. This is going to be your basket handle.

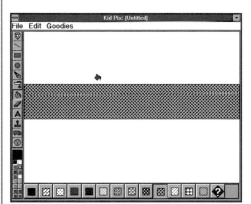

STEP 6 Print it and cut it out. Don't forget to color it.

STEP 7 Use glue, staples or tape and attach the handle to the basket, as this picture shows.

Now you have an Easter basket. Using Kid Pix stamps or drawing tools, you can probably come up with some cool pictures to cut out and paste to your basket; bows, eggs, rabbits, and more. (You're a talented kid—you figure it out.)

More Ideas: Kid Pix can help you make all sorts of Easter decorations; things to hang in windows, Easter cards, and more.

HORRIBLE HALLOWEEN MASKS

Materials needed:
scissors,
crayons/markers/
paint, glue, tape,
string, hole puncher

Kid Pix can help you make great masks for costumes. With a little imagination, you can create some totally awesome masks.

 STEP 1 First you need to design your mask. Do you want to make a scary one? A funny one? A truly bizarre one?

STEP 2 Use Kid Pix to help you create the mask. I made a face mask for my eyes. I started out by making two ovals for eyes. (Actually, I just made one oval, and then copied it using the Moving Van copy trick from Section 3 of this book.) Then I drew shapes around the eyes. It's kind of hard to guess where your eye ovals need to be. You may have to practice to get them in the right place for your own face.

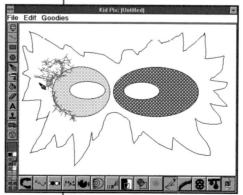

STEP 3 Print out your mask and cut it out.

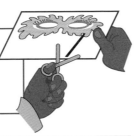

STEP 4 Color your mask using crayons, markers, or paint. You may want to glue on fake beards, moustaches, slimy-scary stuff, whatever. You may also want to glue your mask to stiff construction paper or cardboard— that will make it last longer.

STEP 5 Put two pieces of tape on the back of the mask, right where you want to fasten the ends of the string. (You'll use string or yarn to tie your mask onto your head.) Then use a hole-punch or make two tiny holes in the tape where the string will attach. The tape will make the holes a little stronger.

STEP 6 Use two pieces of string. Tie one end of each string to the holes. Now you have a mask ready to go.

More Ideas: You can use Kid Pix to make masks for any occasion, parties, disguises for secret agent work, and much more. Of course you'll want to make some special masks for scaring your mom or your little brother or sister, right?

53

THANKSGIVING PLACE-SETTING CARDS

Materials needed:
crayons/markers/paint, scissors,
construction paper, glue

Do you have company coming over this Thanksgiving? Give Mom a hand, and help get ready
for that big turkey crowd by making place-setting cards
for the table. (Place-setting cards are like name tags,
except they stand up at each plate to tell who sits
where.) For a funny joke this year, try placing all the
adults' cards at the kids' table, and all the kids' cards
at the adults' table. That will really confuse those
goofy aunts and uncles!

STEP 1 Decide what your place-
setting cards will look like.
Remember, they're just little
name tags that are folded over so they
stand up. So don't make them very big.

STEP 2 Create the cards using Kid
Pix. Here's the pattern I
used to make my cards.

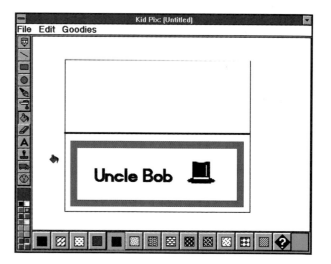

Print out the cards, cut them out, and color them using crayons, markers, or paint. You may even want to glue on glitter, candy corn, turkey feathers, or other "Thanksgiving-y" stuff.

STEP 4

Glue the cards to pieces of stiff construction paper. Fold the cards and place them on the table.

More ideas: You can also make place-setting cards for parties, birthdays, banquets, and other occasions where people have to sit down at a table.

HOLIDAY ORNAMENTS

Materials needed:
scissors, crayons/
markers/paint, tape,
glue, string
Optional: glitter,
ribbon

Make holiday ornaments for decorating the house, the tree, your room, and more.

STEP 1 Decide what kinds of ornaments you will make. I like the simple shapes best, like stars, circles, or pine trees. But with Kid Pix, you can create a whole bunch of holiday things. You can even create shapes for Hanukkah and other religious holidays.

STEP 2 Make your ornaments using the Kid Pix program. Use your Rectangle, Circle, and Line tools to help you.

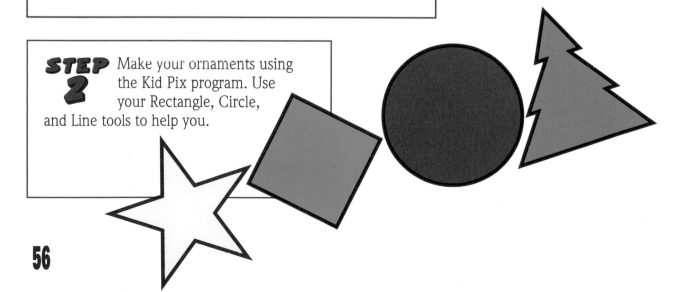

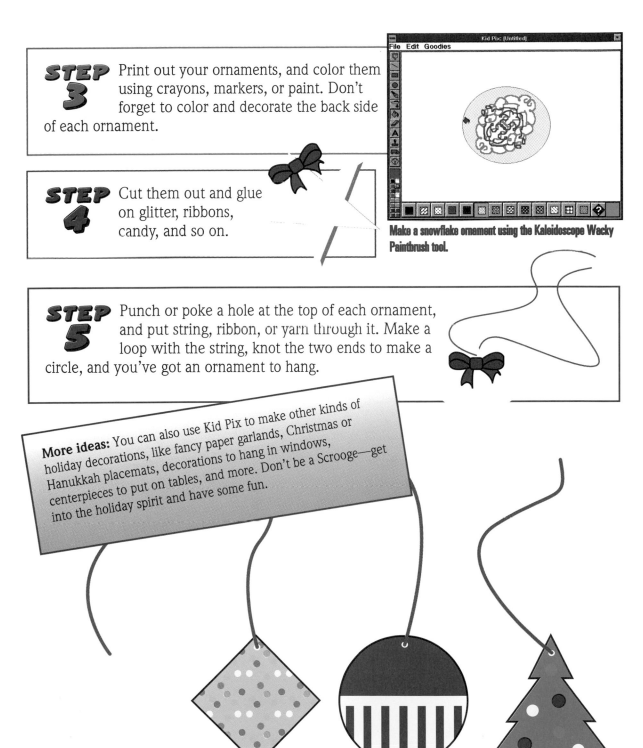

STEP 3 Print out your ornaments, and color them using crayons, markers, or paint. Don't forget to color and decorate the back side of each ornament.

STEP 4 Cut them out and glue on glitter, ribbons, candy, and so on.

Make a snowflake ornament using the Kaleidoscope Wacky Paintbrush tool.

STEP 5 Punch or poke a hole at the top of each ornament, and put string, ribbon, or yarn through it. Make a loop with the string, knot the two ends to make a circle, and you've got an ornament to hang.

More ideas: You can also use Kid Pix to make other kinds of holiday decorations, like fancy paper garlands, Christmas or Hanukkah placemats, decorations to hang in windows, centerpieces to put on tables, and more. Don't be a Scrooge—get into the holiday spirit and have some fun.

Section 6
School Projects

MAKE A MOBILE

Kid Pix can really help you out with school projects and homework. Try out this idea for the next big school project you do—make a mobile. You can make mobiles of the solar system, or plants and animals, or any other subject you study.

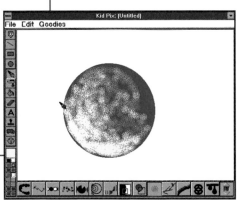

 STEP 1 What's your subject? How many art pieces will you have to make? You have to decide all this before you get started. I'm going to show you how to make a mobile of the solar system. Before I could work on this project, I had to get an encyclopedia to learn about the planets. I had to do research.

STEP 2 Create your mobile art pieces on the computer. After looking at the pictures in the encyclopedia, I knew which planets to draw and how they should look.

STEP 3 Print out your art, and color it using crayons, markers, or paint. You can even glue on fabric, yarn, glitter and other funky art things. Don't forget to color both sides of the art.

STEP 4 Cut out your art and poke holes where each piece will hang. (A hole punch might help.) You may need to glue your art onto a stiffer piece of construction paper.

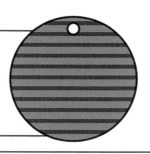

STEP 5 Take string, ribbon, or yarn, and attach one end to the mobile art piece. Attach the other end to a stick or wire, or whatever you're using to hang the mobile from. (You can use a hanger, wooden sticks, popsicle sticks, or pieces of cardboard.)

Hang each art piece separately. Depending on what kind of project you're making, your mobile pieces should be hung differently.

My planets had to be hung in order around the Sun. Once your art is attached, and everything is tied the way you want, hang your mobile and watch it spin. But don't get dizzy.

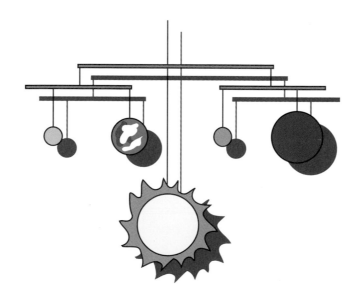

GRAPHS, PIES & CHARTS

Materials needed: crayons/markers/paint

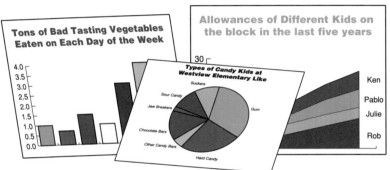

Use Kid Pix to make colorful graphs and charts to illustrate your reports and projects. You might even get an "A" for effort. Just to clue you in, graphs, pies and charts are used to keep track of things. You can use them to measure time, quantities, percentages, just about anything. Of course, you have to know all about what you're keeping track of. That takes a little research, looking things up in books or encyclopedias.

STEP 1 Have all your measurements (or whatever you're keeping track of) written down. For example, my school project was learning about the earth's growing population. I had to find out the population for every 100 years, starting with 1500.

STEP 2 Create your graph, pie or chart using the Kid Pix tools. I decided to make a graph with bars or boxes showing what the earth's population was.

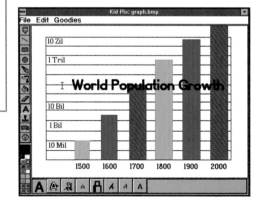

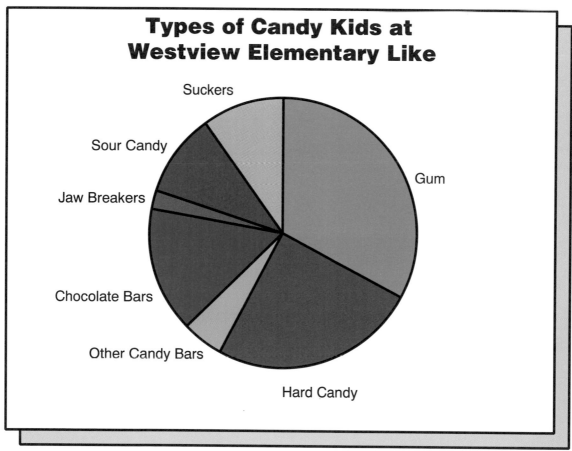

Types of Candy Kids at Westview Elementary Like

Suckers

Sour Candy

Jaw Breakers

Chocolate Bars

Other Candy Bars

Hard Candy

Gum

There—that wasn't so hard to make, was it? Well, I guess that depends on how hard your homework assignment was.

3-D MODELS

You can use Kid Pix to help you create amazing 3-D models of historic places and events. It's a lot of work, but it's also fun. And boy, do they look neat when they're done!

STEP 1 Of course you'll come up with your own ideas, but here's a project I did of George Washington crossing the Delaware River. I used a picture in my history book to help me with this. The first thing I did was sketch out what my 3-D model would look like.

STEP 2 The next thing I did was create the art on Kid Pix. I needed to draw George Washington and his men in a boat, the river with waves of water, and the shore in the back with trees and stuff. I made each part separately.

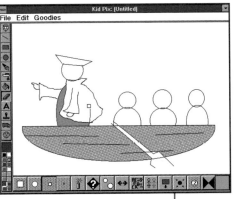

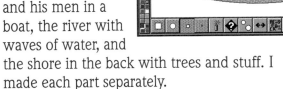

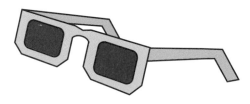

STEP 3 I printed out the art pieces, colored them in and cut them out.

STEP 4 I took a large piece of very stiff construction paper and folded it in half. Then I took my shore and glued it to the construction paper.

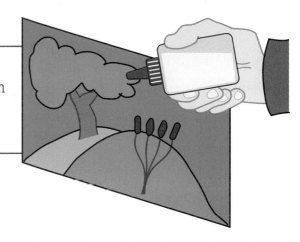

STEP 5 I attached George and his boat to the other fold and bent it to stand up like this picture shows.

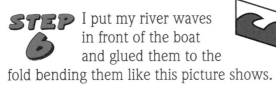

STEP 6 I put my river waves in front of the boat and glued them to the fold bending them like this picture shows.

STEP 7 Now step back and look at the model. It's 3-D! Cool—now you know how to create your own 3-D projects.

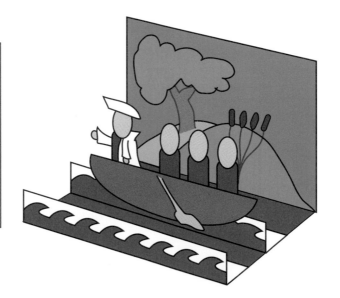

FLAGS

Materials needed:
crayons/markers/paint,
scissors, wooden stick

Here's a fun school project anyone can make. You can use Kid
Pix to make the flags of the world, or invent your own.

 STEP 1 Decide what flag you're going to make, or
come up with a flag of your own. Use an
encyclopedia or history book to help you.

 STEP 2 Use the full Kid Pix
screen to design the flag.

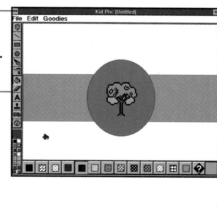

 STEP 3 Print out your
flag, and color it
using crayons,
markers, or paint.

 STEP 4 Cut out your flag.
You can glue it to a
stick or a stiff piece
of cardboard.

Now go fly your
flag!

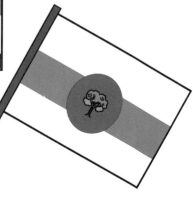

TOTEM POLE

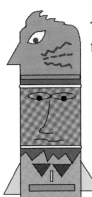

Totem poles were made by Eskimos and American Indians. Get a good book on this subject, and use it to help you make your own Indian totem pole.

STEP 1 Design your totem pole first. What are you going to put on it? How many stacks will it have?

STEP 2 Create each totem pole part separately using Kid Pix.

STEP 3 Print out each part and color it using crayons, markers or paint.

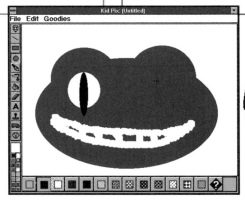

STEP 4 Cut out each part and glue it onto a sturdy piece of cardboard. Don't forget to stack them. Or you can just tape the parts together and hang your totem pole on a wall.

Section 7

Amazing Projects

ACTIVITY BOOKS

Make your own activity books filled with crosswords, dot-to-dots, coloring pages, puzzles, and word games to give to your friends or brothers and sisters. Putting together an activity book is a chance for you to be very creative. Once you're through making a book for everyone else, have them make one for you!

STEP 1 Decide what activities you want to include in your book. It might help to sketch them out before you do them.

STEP 2 Create each activity using the Kid Pix program. Here's what I put in the activity book I made for my friend Bob: a crossword puzzle about comic book heroes, a coloring page with a fish tank, a dot-to-dot of a computer monitor, a scrambled word game, and a hidden pictures puzzle. I also made a title page that says "Spike's Fun Book." Of course, you can come up with all sorts of your own activity pages. Don't forget to make a title page for your book.

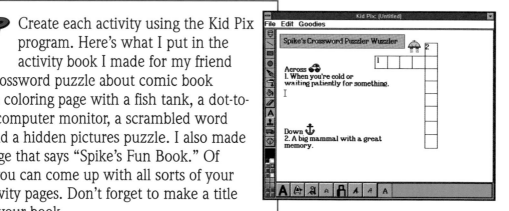

STEP 3

Print out each activity page. You don't have to add color to them if you don't want to. I used markers to color in my title page.

STEP 4

Trim your activity pages using your scissors.

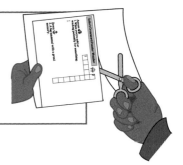

STEP 5

Now you've got to put all your pages together like a book. I used a stapler. You can also use a hole punch, and some string to bind the pages.

Now you've got a great book to give to your friends or brothers and sisters. It will really come in handy on rainy days, long car trips, when they're grounded and have to stay in their room . . . well, you get the idea.

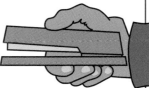

More ideas: Activity books also make great birthday party favors, gifts to send to your pen pals, or you can use them with school projects to help learn about science and history. You can also create story books, picture books, and more using Kid Pix. Maybe this project will make you famous!

Spike's Crossword Puzzler Wuzzler

Across

1. When you're cold or waiting patiently for something.

Down

2. A big mammal with a great memory.

Spike's FUN BOOK

MAKE A PUZZLE

Materials needed: scissors, crayons/markers/paint, stiff construction paper, glue

Use Kid Pix to create puzzles for rainy days—simply use your scissors to cut out the pieces. Then give the pieces to a friend or family member to put together. This doesn't sound too hard, does it?

STEP 1 Decide what your puzzle picture is going to be. You can do a drawing of a scene, like a house on a hill or a forest of trees. You can do wild shapes and colors. You can make your puzzle easy or difficult. But decide all this before you get started.

STEP 2 Create your puzzle on Kid Pix. If you're really clever, you might want to use the Pencil tool to outline your puzzle pieces in black. That will show you where to cut the pieces after you've printed the puzzle out.

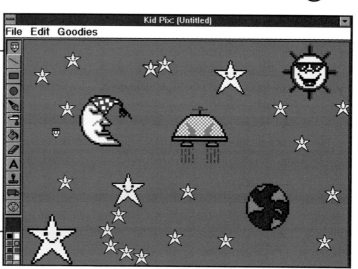

STEP 3 Print out your puzzle, and color it in using crayons, markers, or paint.

STEP 4 To make your puzzle sturdy, you may want to glue it to a stiff piece of construction paper.

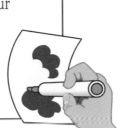

STEP 5 Now cut out each puzzle piece carefully.

STEP 6 Put the pieces into a decorated envelope or small box.

There—now you're ready to give your puzzle to someone to do.

More ideas: You can also create learning puzzles to help you or your friends with math, spelling, science, and more. Use your imagination to see what kinds of puzzles you can come up with.

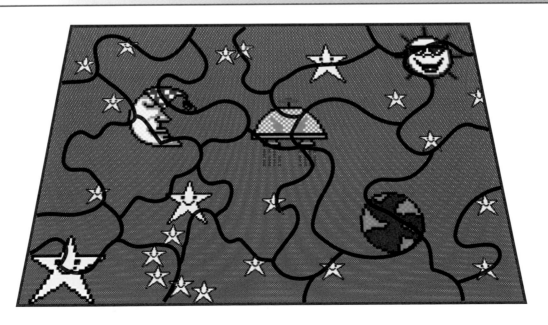

PUPPETS

Kid Pix can help you put together your own puppet show—complete with a cast of characters. You can make finger puppets, string puppets, stick puppets, hand puppets, puppets of every kind! I'm going to show you how to make some finger puppets and perform Shakespeare's "Romeo and Juliet." Just kidding—I'm not going to show you any Shakespeare, just puppets.

STEP 1 Get yourself organized and figure out what kind of puppet characters you're going to make. What do you want them to look like? What will they be wearing? Are they people, animals, robots? Sketch them out if that will help you.

STEP 2 Create each character using your Kid Pix program. I made a family of finger puppet lions. Be sure to leave room to cut a wide band at the bottom of each puppet to fit around your finger.

STEP 3 Print out each puppet and color them in using crayons, markers or paint. You may want to glue your puppets to a stiffer piece of construction paper to make them sturdy.

STEP 4 Cut out each puppet using your scissors.

STEP 5 Decorate the puppets with fabric, yarns, sequins, or beads, whatever you can think of.

STEP 6 Hold the puppet up to your finger and wrap the band around your finger so it fits. Tape or glue the band together to form a circle. Look at this picture to see how I did it.

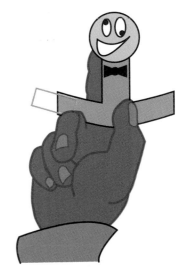

75

COOKBOOK

Materials needed: construction paper, scissors, crayons/markers/paint, glue, stapler or string to bind book

Here's a great idea to help your mom or give as a gift: make recipe cards to put into a book! See how amazing Kid Pix is—it can even help you in the kitchen!

STEP 1 Gather up copies of your favorite recipes. You can make a cookbook with just cookie recipes, sandwich recipes, breakfast recipes, whatever. But first you have to know what's in the recipes. You need ingredients, measurements, cooking time, etc.

STEP 2 Create a card for each recipe using Kid Pix. Type up the ingredients and instructions using the word processor trick from Section 3 of this book. Add some interesting art, or draw what the recipe will look like.

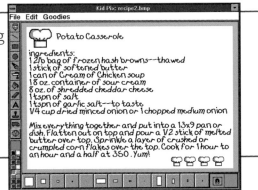

STEP 3 Print out each recipe, and color the drawings in with crayons, markers, or paint.

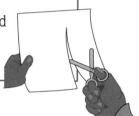

STEP 4 Glue each recipe card to a stiff piece of cardboard or construction paper.

STEP 5 Cut out and trim each card nicely.

STEP 6 Use a hole punch to put holes in the top of each card. Take some string, ribbon, or yarn and tie the cards together. Another way to make your book is to staple all the cards together.

STEP 7 Now give your home-made cookbook to someone to try.

More Ideas: this makes a great idea for a Mother's Day present. Aunts and Grandmas always love cookbooks too. Plus, you can work with your mom to make a "simple" cookbook for your big brother or sister that goes off to college. Throw in a couple of goofy recipes just for fun.

CALENDAR

Materials needed:
scissors, glue or tape, crayons/markers/paint, hole punch and yarn, stapler, construction paper.

Here's an idea from Don Brown at Future Kids in Indianapolis—make your own calendar. Forget about those store-bought calendars, customize your own with Kid Pix. (This is another good gift idea.)

STEP 1 Get a copy of calendar with the correct year. You'll need this to know which dates fall on which days. Watch out for months that have six weeks.
Also: Is your calendar going to have pictures with it? What will be the theme? Animals? Cartoons? Seasons?

STEP 2 Create each month using the Rectangle tool on Kid Pix. Here's a good tip: make a large box with rows of seven boxes across, like this picture.

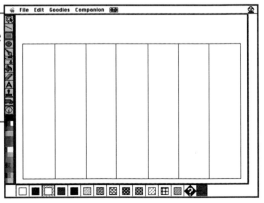

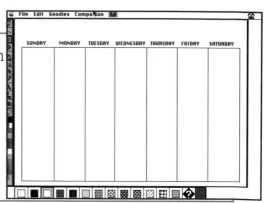

STEP 3 Type up the days of the week and put them at the top of each row where they belong. Be sure to use small letters!

Now save this drawing. Choose **Save As** from the menu. Now name your art. Name it "**Calendar.**" This will be your "master" calendar. You can use this drawing to create each month.

STEP 4 Let's start with January. Count how many weeks are in January. Draw boxes or lines to make those weeks on your screen.

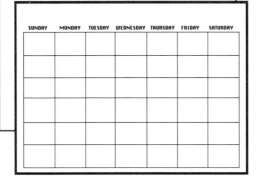

STEP 5 Now put the dates into their correct boxes. You can use the Kid Pix numbers, or make your own number drawings. You can also add art for special days like holidays or birthdays. I like to use the Kid Pix Stamp to mark those days on my calendar.

| JANUARY | | | | | | |
SUNDAY	MONDAY	TUESDAY	WEDNESDAY	THURSDAY	FRIDAY	SATURDAY
					1	2
☀ 3	4	5	6	7	8	9
10	11	12				

STEP 6 Save the month by choosing Save As from the File menu. Type in **January**. Don't worry—you haven't messed up your master calendar. It's still there, in a file called "calendar."

File

	New	⌘N
	Open...	⌘O
	Close	⌘W
	Save	⌘S
	Save As...	
	Page Setup...	
	Print...	⌘P
	Quit	⌘Q

STEP 7 Print out your month, and color it using crayons, markers, or paint.

STEP 8 Trim your calendar using scissors. You may want to glue your calendar to a stiffer piece of construction paper.

Finish the other 11 months by following steps 4–6 for each one.

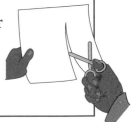

STEP 9 If you are going to draw pictures to go with each month, go back and do those after you have finished making all twelve months.

STEP 10 Put your calendar together using a hole punch and yarn, or staple the pages together. If your calendar has pictures for each month, tape them to the calendar part.

Now you've got a great calendar for your room. Or give it to Mom or Dad to take to the office, hang in the kitchen, or use in the car.

JANUARY

1	2	3	4	5	6	7
8	9	10	11	12	13	14
15	16	17	18	19	20	21
22	23	24	25	26	27	28
29	30	31				

Section 8
Wacky Projects

BONZO BOOKMARKS

Materials needed: construction paper, glue, scissors, crayons/markers/paint
Optional: yarn

Create your own goofy bookmarks to keep or give away as gifts. It's easy and fast using Kid Pix.

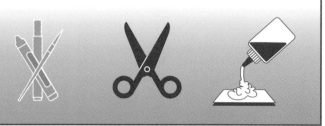

STEP 1 Design your bookmarks on Kid Pix. You can fit several bookmarks on the same screen. I like my book-marks kind of goofy.

STEP 2 Print out your drawing, and color it in using crayons, markers, or paint.

STEP 3 Glue your bookmark to a stiff piece of construction paper.

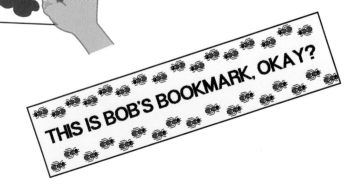
THIS IS BOB'S BOOKMARK, OKAY?

STEP 4 Trim your bookmark using scissors. You may want to add a braided piece of yarn or ribbon to make your bookmark fancier. Now go read a book!

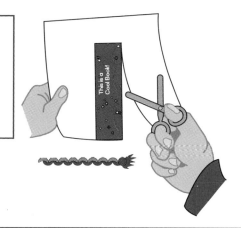

Wow! This was an easy project. Of course, the goofier your bookmarks, the more fun you'll have.

BEWARE of Bookworm

I ♥ to Read

SPIKE'S BOOKMARK
Don't Lose My Place!

BONZO BOOKMARKS (CONT.)

2nd graders Stephanie Luna and Terrance Branch from William McKinley Elementary School #39 in Indianapolis sent me another idea for making bookmarks. I'll share it with you.

STEP 1 First draw two lines on your Kid Pix screen using the Line tool, dividing your screen into 3 equal parts. They can be up and down or across.

STEP 2 Design a different bookmark in each section. Use stamps, letters, and your own pictures.

STEP 3 Print out your designs and color them using crayons, markers or paint.

STEP 4 Cut apart each bookmark on the lines you drew.

STEP 5 Now you can glue them onto cardboard, laminate them or cover them with clear contact paper.

COMIC STRIP

Materials needed: crayons/markers/paint, scissors

Dan Ferrulli, cartoonist, gave me this great idea to use on Kid Pix—design your own comic strip with superheroes or cartoon characters. Maybe this is how Garfield started out . . .

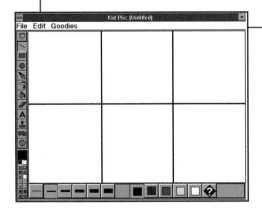

STEP 1 First you have to figure out what kind of comic strip you're going to make. Is it going to be serious or funny? Are you going to use superheroes, animals, people? What's the story or the joke? How many scenes will you need to draw?

The best thing to do is sketch out your ideas.

STEP 2 Use Kid Pix to make your comic strip. Use the Rectangle tool to draw your comic strip boxes. Get as many drawn as you need.

STEP 3 Now fill each box with a scene to tell your story or joke.

STEP 4 Print out your comic strip, and color it in using crayons, markers, or paint.

STEP 5 Trim your comic strip with scissors.

Take a left at the first planet!

Now you're in the funny-papers business.

It was a dark and stormy night at the castle.

No one seemed to be sleeping.

In fact, everyone was up and around!

MAKE A KOOKY KEEP-OUT SIGN

Materials needed: construction paper, crayons/markers/paint, scissors

Hang this project on the door to your room for all to see and read. Keep out! Danger-Radio Active Materials! No Trespassing! Beware of Dog! No Broccoli Allowed! (Get as kooky as you want.)

STEP 1 Create your sign using Kid Pix.

STEP 2 Print out your sign, and color it using crayons, markers, or paint.

STEP 3 Glue your sign to a piece of sturdy construction paper.

STEP 4 Take your scissors and cut out your sign, leaving a hole for it to hang on the doorknob. Follow this picture to see how.

STEP 5 Now hang your sign on your outer doorknob to keep away all intruders. If this doesn't keep people out, then I'll show you how to make barbed wire with Kid Pix. (Not!)

MAKE A KOOKY KEEP-OUT SIGN (CONT.)

Lynn Noel's 2nd graders from William McKinley Elementary School #39 in Indianapolis came up with another way to make a keep out sign.

STEP 1 Use Kid Pix to make your sign. Design it however you want and use the Alphabet stamps to create your words.

STEP 2 Print out your sign and color it in using crayons, markers or paint.

STEP 3 Trim your sign and glue the sign onto stiff cardboard, laminate it or cover it with clear contact paper.

STEP 4 Punch 2 holes at the top of the sign.

 STEP 5 Cut a piece of yarn 8 inches long.

 STEP 6 Put the yarn through the holes and tie a knot with the ends.

Now your sign is ready to hang. Thanks Larry Ross, Nygree Ogletree, and Cassie Noland for sending me your sign ideas! I really liked yours, Cassie—"Stay Out—No Boys Allowed." I guess that means me.

MY OWN MONEY

Materials needed: crayons/markers/paint, scissors

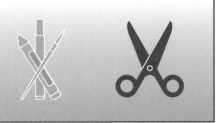

Here's an idea from Karen Hanckel and the Education Department at Future Kids. Design your own play money, with you as president! Give them to friends and family to "spend." They can use them to buy help with chores, cleaning up rooms, washing cars, mowing lawns, babysitting, etc.

STEP 1 Design your money using the Kid Pix program. Draw a nice big rectangle, then add art (a picture of you in the middle, money amounts, historic buildings, whatever).

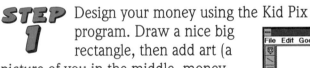

STEP 2 Print out your money, and color it in using crayons, markers, or paint.

STEP 3 Trim your money using scissors.

Tip 1: If you want a backside to your paper money, just design it, print it out, color it and glue it to your front side.

Tip 2: If you have a scanner hooked up to your computer, you could scan in a photo of yourself and put your picture on your money. Ask your mom or dad to help you with this.

MONEY

MY MONEY

More ideas: You can make different amounts of money to help your younger brother or sister learn to add and subtract money.

AMAZING MAPS

Materials needed: crayons/markers/paint, scissors

Make a map to your house to give to friends or relatives. This is a great idea from Don Brown at Future Kids in Indianapolis, Indiana.

STEP 1 Draw a sketch of what your map will look like. Make sure you have all the directions right. Include some landmarks, like big buildings, schools, parks, funny signs.

STEP 2 Use Kid Pix to create your map. The Straight Line tool will really help you draw streets. The Stamp tool can help you add trees and buildings.

STEP 3 Print out your map, and color it in using crayons, markers, or paint.

Now you can give it to anyone who needs to find their way to your house.

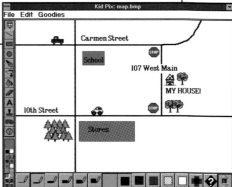

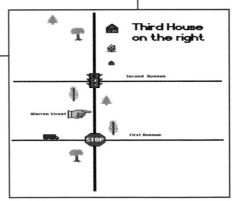

Section 9
Totally Radical
Projects

ACTION FIGURES

Materials needed: construction paper, crayons/markers/paint, scissors, glue, cardboard

Create your own paper action figures using Kid Pix, then use your imagination to play with them. I'll show you how to make them stand up with cardboard props, then you can figure out how to knock them down! (That's why they call them "action" figures, isn't it?)

STEP 1 First decide what kind of action figures you're going to make. Army soldiers? Monsters? Robots? Superheroes? How many will you make?

STEP 2 Create each one using Kid Pix to help you. I made some monster figures myself. I used the Circle and the Rectangle tools to make the bodies, then I drew faces and stuff.

STEP 3 Print out your action guys or gals, and color them in using crayons, markers, or paint.

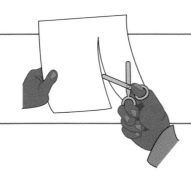

STEP 4 Glue the action figures onto stiff construction paper, and then cut them out.

STEP 5 Finally, make a cardboard stand to prop your figures up. Here's how I made mine. I took a piece of cardboard and folded it. I glued one side to the action figure. Look at this picture to see how it works.

Now you can create armies of men, monsters, outer space creatures, and more.

The Purple Knight

PAPER DOLLS

Materials needed: construction paper, scissors, glue, crayons/markers/paint, cardboard
Optional: fabric scraps, yarn, bows, glitter, sequins, buttons

Make your own paper dolls and clothes for hours of play.

STEP 1 Decide what kind of paper doll you're going to create and what kind of clothes it will wear. You might want to sketch out what you would like it to look like.

STEP 2 Design the doll using the Kid Pix program. I used the Circle tool to make the doll body. Then I added eyes and a face. Make sure you save the first doll—you'll use it to help design the clothing. To save your doll drawing, choose **Save As** from the **File** menu. Name your file "**Doll**" or something you'll remember.

STEP 3 Print out the paper doll, and use crayons, markers, or paint to add color.

STEP 4 Glue the doll to a stiff piece of construction paper or cardboard. Then use your scissors to cut out the shape.

You may want to glue on yarn for hair, fabric pieces, craft eyes, or other things to make your doll interesting.

STEP 5 Next, make a doll stand out of folded cardboard. Look at the doll stand I made to help you. Glue your stand to the doll.

STEP 6 Now go back to the Kid Pix program and design some clothes for your doll to wear. Use the doll you made in step 2 and saved on a Kid Pix file. If you want to save each outfit you design, just choose **Save As** from the **File** menu and give the clothes a name. That way you won't change anything permanently on the first doll.

STEP 7 Print out each outfit, color it using crayons, markers, or paint. You may even want to glue on fabric, buttons, sequins, or beads.

STEP 7 Now cut out your doll outfit, but leave square tabs so you can fold them onto your paper doll. Look at this picture to help you.

Now that you know how to make a computer paper doll, you can create lots of them to play with.

BIRTHDAY PARTY KIT

Materials needed:
construction paper, glue, scissors, string, crayons/markers/paint, tape

Who would have thought of using Kid Pix to make a birthday party kit—design hats, invitations, place-settings, decorations, and more? Well, I did! Now let me show you how to do it.

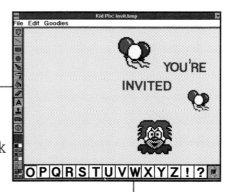

STEP 1 The invitation. This one's easy, just use Kid Pix to type up and design a party invitation. Use the card-making steps back on page 48 about valentines.

STEP 2 The hat. Every party needs hats. Create a funky design on Kid Pix, print it out and color it, make it into a cone, glue or tape it, punch holes for strings to tie the hat on. Easy. Follow the steps in this picture.

STEP 3 Placemats. Another easy one. Make a cool design for birthday placemats using Kid Pix. Print them out and color them, set them on the table, and you're ready to party.

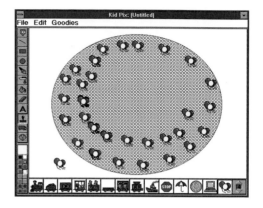

STEP 4 The decorations. I used circle designs I created on Kid Pix, printed them out and cut them in spirals to make hanging decorations. Follow this picture to see how I did it.

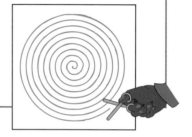

You can also use Kid Pix to help you make paper chains, "Happy Birthday" posters, centerpieces, and all sorts of creative stuff.

How's that for a birthday party kit?

TREASURE MAP

Materials needed: crayons/markers/paint

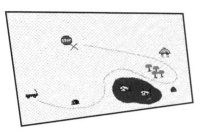

Here's a fun game you can play with your friends or your brothers and sisters. "Bury" (or hide) a "treasure," and make a map for someone to follow to find the treasure!

STEP 1 Make a plan, decide what the treasure will be. Candy? A toy? Coins? Carefully hide the treasure so no one can see it. If it's nice outside, hide it in the backyard. If it's rainy, hide it inside the house. (Make sure it's okay with your parents first.)

STEP 2 Make a map using Kid Pix with mysterious clues to help the reader find the treasure. I used the Rubber Stamps to stand for certain things—like the footsteps or arrow stamps showing which way to go.

STEP 3 Print out your map, and color it using crayons, markers, or paint.

STEP 4 Now give it to someone to track down the treasure!

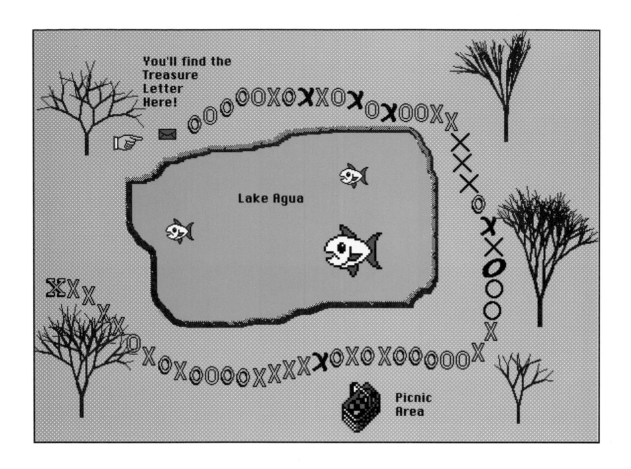

CAUTION—don't hide anything that might melt (like chocolate) if it's not found soon! And don't forget where you "buried" the treasure yourself!

Section 10
Projects to do
Using Kid Pix
Companion

If you have the Kid Pix Companion program on your computer, you can do the projects in this section. If you don't have Kid Pix Companion, I'll tell you what it is. (That's because I'm such a nice guy.)

Kid Pix Companion is an extra program you can buy for your computer. You can make computer slide shows with it. (The Mac version even has animation stuff!) Slide shows are like movies, but with pictures that hold still. Pictures you make on Kid Pix show up on the computer screen to look at, one at a time. It's a lot of fun. Kid Pix Companion even lets you add sounds to your show, or record your own voice! I'll bet Steven Spielberg didn't have this when he was a kid!

How It Works

If you have Kid Pix Companion, let's go into the SlideShow program now. (If you're in the middle of Kid Pix, quit the program by choosing **Quit** from the **File** menu.)

To use the SlideShow, Mac users should look for the SlideShow icon and double-click it on when you find it (just like you double-click to get into Kid Pix). If you're using IBM, type **Show** at the DOS prompt (c:> SHOW), but make sure you're in the Kid Pix directory.

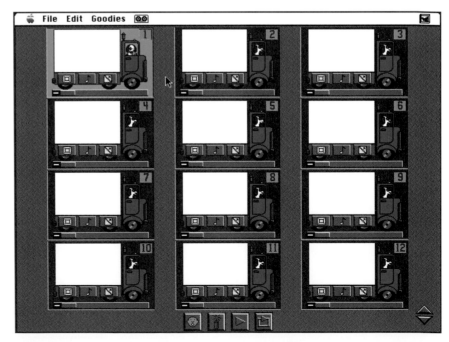

(IBM users—there's also a shortcut to the SlideShow on the Companion menu in Kid Pix.) When your program starts, you'll see lots of little trucks on the screen. All those little trucks in the picture are slides. You can make up to 99 slides! That's a lot of pictures. Notice each slide truck has a number. That's what order the pictures will be shown in when you start the show.

You can move these trucks around to change their order. Just click on the picture you want to move, hold down the mouse button, and move the mouse to where you want the picture to go.

Another Menu, Please!

At the top of the screen is a menu bar. Most of these menus are the same as in Kid Pix, but some have menu items that will help you create your slide show.

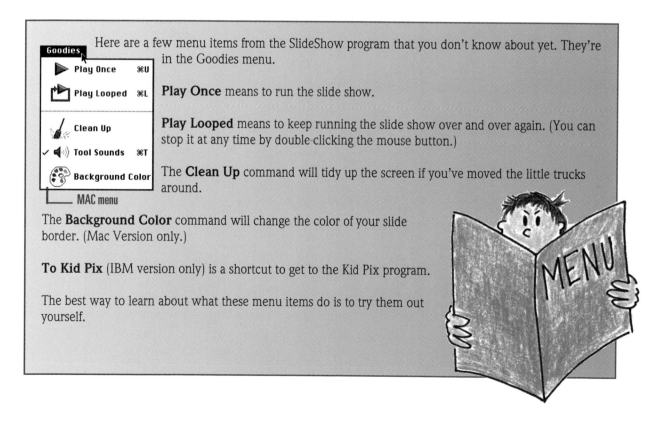

Here are a few menu items from the SlideShow program that you don't know about yet. They're in the Goodies menu.

Play Once means to run the slide show.

Play Looped means to keep running the slide show over and over again. (You can stop it at any time by double-clicking the mouse button.)

The **Clean Up** command will tidy up the screen if you've moved the little trucks around.

The **Background Color** command will change the color of your slide border. (Mac Version only.)

To Kid Pix (IBM version only) is a shortcut to get to the Kid Pix program.

The best way to learn about what these menu items do is to try them out yourself.

Boffo Buttons

Look at a slide truck.

 At the bottom of the truck are some control buttons. The left control button lets you pick which picture file you want to make into a slide. Just click on the button with your mouse pointer. Choose the file you want to be in the slide. Click the **Select** button, and you've chosen a picture!

The middle button lets you pick sounds to go with your slide, or record your own. That means you can narrate a story you draw (if you have a computer system with a microphone)! This is so cool!

The right button lets you choose how you want your picture to come and go on the computer screen. You can **fade out** to the next slide, or **dissolve** your picture. (These are fancy "special effects" words that they use in making movies!)

The little bar at the bottom of each slide helps you tell how many seconds the slide stays on the screen before the next one is shown. (It depends on what sounds you've put with each slide.)

At the very bottom of your SlideShow screen are four more buttons to use. The Undo Guy and the Firecracker stick work the same way as they do in the Kid Pix drawing program. The other two buttons play your slide show. The two triangle buttons at the far bottom right of your screen will let you move up and down to see the other slides (up to number 99).

Now that you know about the SlideShow program, it's time to try a few projects. I've got some awesome ideas that you're going to flip over! Or at least do a backbend.

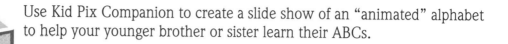

ANIMATED ALPHABET

Use Kid Pix Companion to create a slide show of an "animated" alphabet to help your younger brother or sister learn their ABCs.

STEP 1 Use the Kid Pix program first. I stamped alphabet letters on the screen one at a time. Each time I stamped a letter, I saved the picture using **Save As** from the **File** menu. I named the first picture file **ALPH1**. Each time I added a letter I saved it, giving it a new ALPH name (ALPH2, ALPH3, etc.).

Every time I added a letter, I also stamped a picture of something that started with that letter, or drew a new picture. I saved this screen too.

I did this for all 26 letters of the alphabet. That means I saved 52 files! (52 because I saved 26 screens with letters on them, and 26 screens with pictures on them.) I'm not going to show you all of those, but I'll show you the first four.

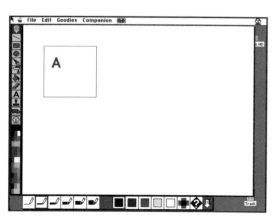

Start with the letter **A**. Stamp it at the top of your screen. I put a big box around mine.

Now save your picture using **Save As** from the **File** menu. Name the file ALPH1.

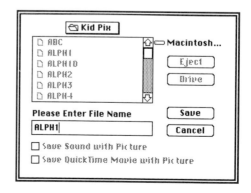

Next, use the Rubber Stamp to put an apple next to the A.

Now save your picture again. This time name it **ALPH2**.

Stamp the letter **B** on your screen. Save it as **ALPH3**.

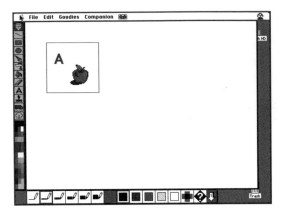

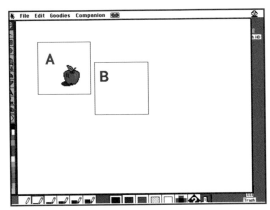

Now find a Rubber Stamp that starts with the letter B. How about a bird? Stamp the bird next to the letter B and save your picture. Name it **ALPH4**.

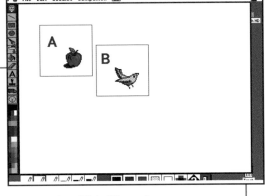

 After you've made all your picture files and saved them on Kid Pix, choose **Quit** from the **File** menu.

STEP 3 Open up the Slide-Show program. (IBM users can use the shortcut in the Companion menu to get to the SlideShow.)

STEP 4 Now it's time to put your alphabet slide show together. Use the command buttons (we went over them at the beginning of this section) to help you place each alphabet letter and picture into your slide show. Don't forget to use special effects and sound with your show!

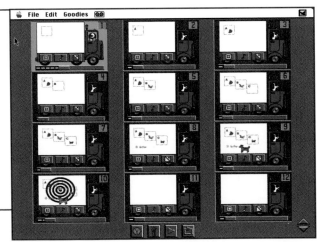

LEARN TO SPEAK SPANISH

Make a slide show that translates words from English to Spanish. This is a great way to teach a foreign language.

STEP 1 Plan which words or sentences you would like to make. Write out the English and Spanish words. You might want to get a dictionary to help you. Also plan what pictures you would like to put with the words. I used the Rubber Stamp pictures to illustrate my translation.

> English

STEP 2 Create each picture using Kid Pix, and save each one using the **Save As** command from the **File** menu. Here's how I made mine.

> English
> Inglés

First I wrote the word in English. I used the Kid Pix word processor trick (from Section 3 of this book) to help me. Then I saved the screen using **Save As** from the **File** menu.

Next, I wrote the word in Spanish underneath the English version. Then I saved the screen again.

Finally, I stamped a picture of the word, or drew a new picture to go with the word. I saved this screen too.

I repeated all these steps to make each of my slides.

STEP 3 After you've made all your picture files and saved them on Kid Pix, choose **Quit** from the **File** menu. (IBM users can take the shortcut in the Companion menu.)

 **STEP 4** Open up the SlideShow program.

STEP 5 Now it's time to put your language translation slide show together. Use the command buttons described at the beginning of this section to help you place each word and picture onto your slide show.

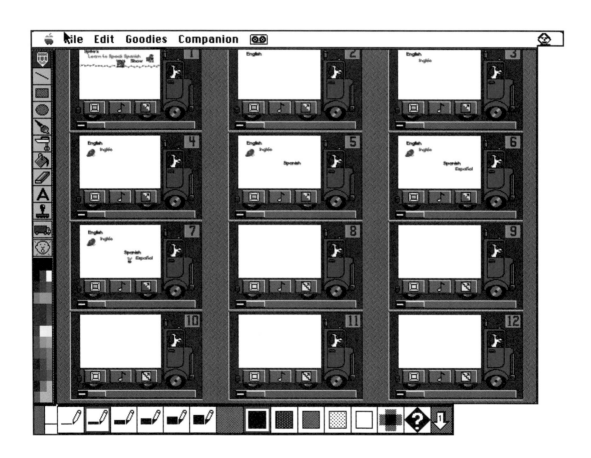

CONNECT THE DOTS

Use the SlideShow feature to create a connect-the-dots show! You can make a line magically appear to connect each dot. Here's how.

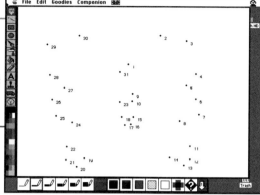

STEP 1 Create a dot-to-dot picture using the Wacky Paint Brush's Dot-to-dot tool. Make sure all the connecting lines are gone when you finish the drawing.

STEP 2 Save the picture using the **Save As** command from the **File** menu. Now go back and use the Straight Line tool to connect dot 1 to dot 2. Save this screen. Then repeat until you connect all the dots.

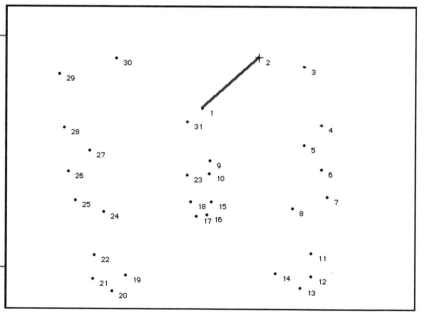

STEP 3 After you've made all your picture files and saved them on Kid Pix, choose **Quit** from the **File** menu. (IBM users can use the shortcut on the Companion menu.)

STEP 4 Open up the SlideShow program.

STEP 5 Now it's time to put your dot-to-dot slide show together. Use the command buttons to help you place each word and picture into your slide show.

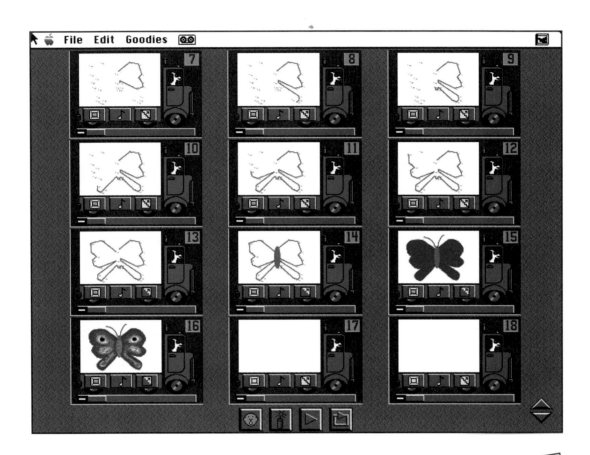

More ideas: You can also do this to make cartoons seem to draw themselves!

SLIDE SHOW BOOK REPORT

Kid Pix Companion can help you put together a really cool book report!

STEP 1 Plan out how you would like each page to look. What words and what pictures will go on each page? Once you've figured all that out, you can get started on Kid Pix.

STEP 2 Make a title page for your report. Then save it using the **Save** command from the **File** menu.

STEP 3 Starting with Page Two of your report, type up the words and draw a picture for that page using the Kid Pix program. Then save it using the **Save** command from the **File** menu.

This book is about a girl named Alice who falls down a hole. She meets up with many strange characters. The first one is a rabbit.

STEP 4 Open a new page for Page Three. Now make Page Three on your Kid Pix screen. Repeat all these steps to finish the report.

STEP 5 After you've made all your picture files and saved them on Kid Pix, choose **Quit** from the **File** menu. (IBM users can use the shortcut on the Companion menu.)

STEP 6 Open up the SlideShow program.

STEP 7 Now it's time to put your book report slide show together. Use the command buttons at the beginning of this section to help you place each page into your slide show. Boy, is your teacher going to be impressed!

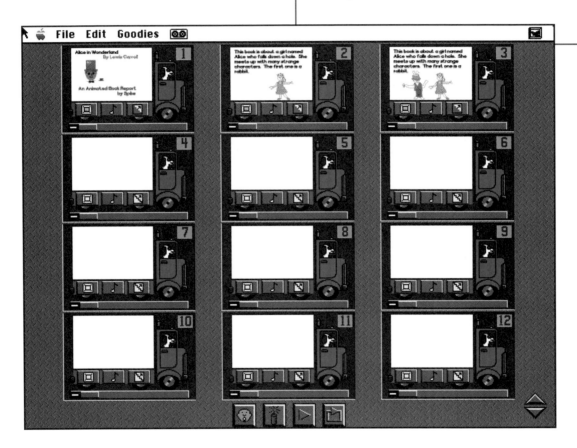

Section 11
More
Projects

MORE PROJECTS!

Just in case you were wondering what else you can do with Kid Pix, here are some more great ideas. Look for family projects, class projects, science projects, things to do on your own, play kits, dress up kits, run your own business, art stuff, dollhouse fun, games, all kinds of cards, putting on a play, animal menageries, more holiday ideas, practical crafts, clubs and teams, delinquent projects, gift ideas, and around the world with Kid Pix.

Family Time

Projects you can make with your entire family.

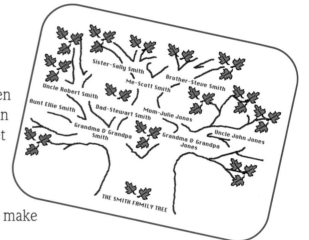

Family Tree—Use Kid Pix to help you illustrate a family tree to trace your personal history. You can even draw pictures of what each relative looks like. You can also make a form on Kid Pix to send to relatives to get important family history information, like who married who and on what date, where they were born, what color eyes, etc. Once you've collected all the pictures and information, use Kid Pix to help you make a giant tree to paste everything onto.

Family Games—Use Kid Pix to make board games for your family and friends to play. You can design the playing pieces, spinning wheel, question cards, and more! Glue everything to stiff construction paper or cardboard, and you're ready to play. Of course, you'll have to come up with your own rules. That could be fun—a rule that says you always win!

Family Phone Lists—Use Kid Pix to help you create your own phone directory. Use the word processing trick in Section 3 to type everything in, then illustrate your directory using Kid Pix stamps and artwork. Place the directory by the phone so everyone can use it.

Design a Family Crest—You can draw and design your own family crest, just like royal families in Europe have. And if your family ever needs a neat design to put on a shield of armor, you'll have one all set to go! Of course, you can also use your crest to decorate, put on your front door or mailbox, paste on family albums, and so on.

Create Your Own Family Newsletter—With Kid Pix, you can put together a newsletter of interesting activities, events, birthdays, and exciting things you and your family are up to. Then you can send it to friends and relatives.

Seasonal Tree—Make a tree to decorate every season. (Trees aren't just for Christmas, you know.) Take a stick with lots of branches and stand it upright in a container of rocks or sand. Now you and your family can decorate it each season using decorations you make on Kid Pix. Try a Valentine tree, an Easter tree… maybe even a Columbus Day tree! This will make a great centerpiece!

Vacation Memories—Illustrate your recent vacation using Kid Pix. Make an itinerary of everywhere you went, drawing pictures of each place. Each family member can illustrate his or her favorite part of the vacation.

Vacation Slides—Forget about those real slides! If you have the Kid Pix Companion program on your computer, you can use Kid Pix to make a slide show of your most recent vacation. You and your family can take turns drawing and adding music or narration.

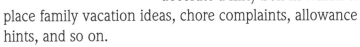

Make a Family Suggestion Box—Use Kid Pix to inspire and decorate a nifty box in which to place family vacation ideas, chore complaints, allowance hints, and so on.

Allowance Reminder Slips—Does your family have a tough time keeping track of allowances? Use Kid Pix to help you get organized. You can make a great chart. You can also design some cool reminder slips to hand out on "Pay Day"!

Class Time

Kid Pix projects are fun for the whole class.

Weatherman Charts—Kid Pix can help your class keep track of weather, temperatures, rainfall, and more. Turn your students into weather reporters in no time!

Weather Maps—Use Kid Pix to help students track weather. Import maps from other drawing programs and use Kid Pix art to follow the latest weather reports from around the world. This is a great project for building your own weather studio!

Junior Geographers—Use Kid Pix to help your class study geography and history maps. Kids can design their own planets, countries, and maps.

Arty Architects—Use Kid Pix to create building plans and layouts. Kids can design their own city maps with traffic flow, buildings, parks, sewer systems and recycling plants, electrical plants, and more.

Dance Steps—Help your class learn the latest dance steps or square dance moves. Use Kid Pix to design footsteps to place on the floor!

Musically Inclined—Design sheet music and notes on Kid Pix! Kid Pix can help students learn notes and songs, and learn to read music, memorize piano keys, and more.

Rebus Stories—Kid Pix stamps are perfect for putting together Rebus stories. (Rebus stories use pictures instead of words.) Use with the Kid Pix word processing trick, and you have a creative writing class ready to go!

Make Your Own Dictionary—Kids are good at inventing their own words! Now Kid Pix can help you make an illustrated dictionary. What a great way to study phonetics, language skills, and spelling!

Time Ticks Away—Use Kid Pix to help students learn to tell time. Kids can design their own clocks with working hands!

Science Projects

Kid Pix can help with any science project from charts, to posters, to diagrams, and more!

Electrified Charts—Use Kid Pix to help students study and chart the flow of electricity.

Sail into the Solar System—Create planets, stars, spacecraft, satellites, and more. Kid Pix can help classes study the universe, space travel, comets, and all kinds of cool stuff.

 Animal Life—Use Kid Pix to chart and diagram animals from around the world. You can even make animal cutouts.

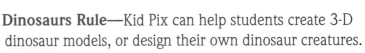 **Dinosaurs Rule**—Kid Pix can help students create 3-D dinosaur models, or design their own dinosaur creatures.

Design Your Own Species—Use Kid Pix to help students create and plan their own animal species. Omnivore or herbivore, mammal or fish, kids can study how animals survive in different environments and climates.

Things to Do on Your Own

 **Make a Diary**—Use Kid Pix to write up diary pages to print out and save in a notebook. You can even illustrate them!

Make an Address Book—Type up your friends addresses using the word processing trick in section 3, add some artwork, and design your own address book using Kid Pix.

Make Some Rules—Create a poster of rules for your bedroom, your house, your club, your class. Type up your list and decorate it with Kid Pix art.

Make a Chart—Track your household chores and personal progress activities. You can make all sorts of charts using Kid Pix to keep track of chores, teeth-brushing, nail-biting, room-cleaning, book-reading, etc.

Play Kits

Do you like to play things like office, restaurant, bank, school, library, spies, travel agent, detective? You know, imaginary games? Good, then these ideas are for you.

Make Your Own Spy Kit—Use the computer to help you create nifty disguises like glasses, moustaches, paper wigs, hats, and more. Build yourself some paper binoculars, secret weapons, and top secret briefcases.

Office Kit—Print out special forms, stationery, envelopes, stamps, desk calendars, telephone message pads, or company invoices. With Kid Pix, you can even build a paper telephone, a pretend typewriter and much, much more!

Restaurant Kit—Planning on opening a restaurant? Make your own menus, order tickets, paper hats and aprons. You can even make play plates, cups, forks, and spoons! And don't forget to make a sign for your restaurant.

Make a Bank—Print out your own play money, coins, checks, deposit slips, and more. With Kid Pix, you can make signs, pretend credit cards, even name badges.

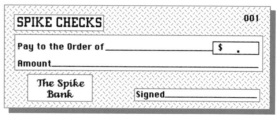

Travel Agent Kit—Are you "working" in a travel agency? Kid Pix can help you make signs, airline tickets, play money, name tags, and more. Don't forget to make passports for those far away trips!

Running a Hospital—You'll need lots of forms, patient I.D. bracelets, X-rays, pretend tools, medical charts, nurses hats, stethoscopes, and other medical stuff. Don't forget to make some bills!

Kid Pix can help you make play kits for any imaginary game.

Dress Up Kits

Do you like to pretend you're someone else? Do you like to wear disguises? Then try these dress up ideas using Kid Pix.

Prince or Princess—Use Kid Pix to help you make crowns, jewelry, and more. You can make all kinds of paper diamond rings, necklaces, bracelets, and other fun things to wear. Do royalty wear paper watches?

Cheerleading—Create your own pom-poms, team letters to pin on your cheerleading outfit, team logos, pennants, and sports stuff.

Cowboys and Indians, Cops and Robbers—Kid Pix can help you make all kinds of hats, feathers, badges, and weapons.

Hats, Hats, Hats—You can create all sorts of hats using Kid Pix: sun visors, chef's hats, sailor's hats, ladies hats, soldier hats, sport hats. Just use your imagination to put your hats together, or put your heads together to make hats. Whatever.

Space Crafts—Are you visiting from another planet? Design your own space helmet, spaceship control board, rocket gun, and more.

Run Your Own Business

Here are some awesome ideas for kids starting their own businesses.

Lemonade Stand Kit—Kid Pix can help you put together a great lemonade stand. Use your computer to make signs, price menus, hats, name badges, receipts, flyers to pass out to the neighborhood, and posters to pin up on poles and bulletin boards.

Lawn Mowing Man—Design flyers and posters advertising your lawn mowing business. Pass them out to neighbors or nail them on poles. You can also use Kid Pix to help you make forms to keep track of your customers and your money. You can even make a lawn-mowing schedule.

Make Your Own Business Cards—Create business cards to pass out to friends, neighbors, and customers. Be sure to include your name, telephone number, and hours you can work.

Business Logos—You can use your computer to design logos for your business. Logos are pictures that go with your company name. Sometimes they show what your company does. Sometimes they just look neat!

Paperboy Papers—Have you got a paper route that's hard to keep track of? Use Kid Pix to create a chart to keep track of money, addresses, names, and more. You can also use Kid Pix to help you advertise.

Art Stuff

Feeling kind of artsy? Kid Pix can help you create some awesome art to hang, give as gifts, or keep in your own art gallery.

Designer Paper Chains—You know the paper chains you make at school out of construction paper? Well, now you can design your own using Kid Pix stamps and letters. String them up in your room, or use as party decorations.

Relief Prints—Create 3-D crafts using Kid Pix to help. Print out several copies of the same picture. Cut out parts and glue them onto the original picture in layers. This will make them stick up. This art technique is called relief art.

Collage—Make a Kid Pix collage of art, shapes, and colors.

Stuffed Paper Sculptures—Your computer can help you create sculptures of animals, objects, dinosaurs, machines, and more. Design a pattern for the front and back and print them out. Glue or tape them together and stuff with paper. Voila! A sculpture!

Paint-by-Numbers—Make your own paint by number sheets to give to family or friends. It's easy and fun with Kid Pix.

Dollhouse Fun

Have you got a dollhouse? Kid Pix can help you decorate.

Wallpaper—Use Kid Pix to design your own dollhouse wallpaper patterns. Then cut them out and glue them on.

Paintings and Pictures—Create lots of little paintings and pictures to hang on your dollhouse walls, on the fireplace mantel, and more.

Furniture—You can think up all kinds of furniture to make using Kid Pix. You can even make rugs for the floors and curtains for the windows.

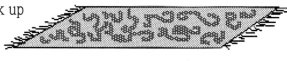

Games

Make your own game boards, cards, and more. Give them as gifts, or use them for travel games during long car trips. Try making your own Trivial Pursuit or Monopoly games.

Bingo—Kid Pix can help you design your own Bingo cards, cover chips, and number callouts.

Playing Cards—Design your own playing cards for card games and board games.

Travel Games—Make up your own travel games using Kid Pix to help you illustrate and design. Try checkerboards, Tic Tac Toe sheets, Hangman forms, and more.

Do-It-Yourself Stationery

Do you love getting mail? Try sending some — it's great with Kid Pix!

Letterhead—Make your own personalized paper for writing letters to friends and family.

Greeting Cards—Create dozens of holiday and birthday cards for you and your family to mail.

Thank Yous—Whip up special thank you notes to send to Grandma and Grandpa, or Aunt Edna who knitted you that swell scarf for Christmas.

All Kinds of Cards

Ralph Lamotta

Statistics: age 8, missing one front tooth, favorite hobbies include video games, playing army and eating dirt. Height 3'2"

There are all sorts of cards around today. Now you can make your own. Try some of these . . Greeting Cards, Thank You Cards, Holiday Cards—You can design all sorts of cards to give to family and friends.

Collector's Cards—Make your own neighborhood collector's cards. Sort of like baseball cards, you draw pictures of the neighborhood kids and include their vital statistics (height, weight, favorite foods, sports, classes, and so on). You could even include a stick of gum!

Report Cards—Make up your own school report cards with wacky classes and grades.

Putting On a Play

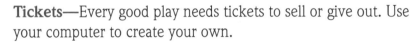

Kid Pix can help with your next theater play. Try these project ideas . . . .

Tickets—Every good play needs tickets to sell or give out. Use your computer to create your own.

Advertising—Make flyers, posters, signs, and invitations to give to neighbors, friends, and family.

Scripts and Cue Cards—Write up your scripts using Kid Pix. Or make large signs with the words to the play to help people who don't memorize very well.

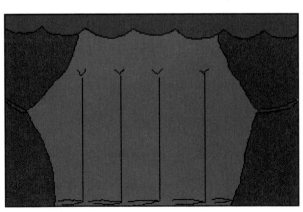

Playbills—Make your own pamphlet describing your play, the actors, and the sets, to hand out to the audience.

Menageries

Use your computer to build entire collections of zoo animals, army men, farm animals, villages, moonbases, and more.

Make a Zoo—Design your animals, print them out, color and cut them, and glue them onto stands or other craft items, and you've got a zoo. You can even build cages and sets to house your animals.

Down on the Farm—Make farm animals, tractors, and barns to build your own farm set. You can even design fences, fields of crops, and more.

Make a Moonbase—Engineer your own space machines, dome buildings, spacemen, and more. Create a landing strip, an orbiting space station, or some crazy moon monsters.

Noah's Ark—Craft your own Noah's ark complete with animals and boat. Kid Pix can help you be creative and maybe even make a flood!

Indian Village—Complete with teepees, tomahawks, totem poles, and more. Create a miniature village using Kid Pix art and tools.

More Holiday Ideas

You may never run out of holiday ideas to make with Kid Pix. How about some of these?

Paper Stockings—Hang on the tree, as decorations, or even on the fireplace mantel. Print out two identical copies, glue or tape them along the edges, decorate, and hang. A real stocking! That was easy!

Christmas Luminaries—Use Kid Pix to help you make cutout patterns for luminary bags. (Luminaries are bags or containers with candles burning inside. People place them outside on sidewalks and steps.)

Design Your Own Halloween Bags—Make them scary, make them fun, make them all yourself. Kid Pix art can make you the most creative goblin on the block.

Snowy Snowflakes—Use Kid Pix to design special snowflakes to decorate your windows and doors.

Wacky Doggie Antlers—Create and cut out designer antlers to turn any dog into a reindeer. Be sure to glue your antlers to stiff cardboard, then staple or glue them to a stiff cardboard band to fit on Fido's head. Be careful and don't get bit!

Pumpkin Carving Patterns—Why settle for an ordinary jack-o-lantern this year? Use Kid Pix art to design a perfect pumpkin.

Angelic Angels—Put together your own computer angels. Add wings and string to hang about the house.

Paper Webs and Spiders—What better way to decorate for Halloween? Design and cut out interesting webs and spiders to hang from them.

Holiday Buttons—Make fun and clever holiday buttons to pin on friends, teachers, and family. Don't forget about St. Patricks day, Valentine's Day, April Fool's Day, Mother's Day, and Father's Day.

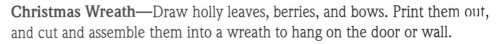

Christmas Advent Calendar—Create your own Christmas countdown calendar to reveal a surprise each day.

Holiday Mail—Kid Pix can help you write and illustrate letters to Santa, the Easter Bunny, even Mr. Groundhog on Groundhog's day.

Christmas Wreath—Draw holly leaves, berries, and bows. Print them out, and cut and assemble them into a wreath to hang on the door or wall.

Easter Egg Stands—Make circular bands to hold hard-boiled Easter eggs. Kid Pix can make them pretty, funny, or pretty funny.

Practical Crafts

I'll bet you can think up all sorts of things that need labels. Try out some of these projects:

Gardening Labels—Use Kid Pix and wooden popsicle sticks to make creative labels for your family garden. Don't forget to laminate them or put plastic over them to keep out water.

Book Covers—Got a notebook or folder that's wearing out? Need to protect a new book you just bought? Use Kid Pix to make a nifty book cover to protect it.

Personal Belongings Labels—Use Kid Pix to make labels such as: Belongs To, Property of, or Please Return to. Stick them in books, lunchboxes, toys—anywhere.

Name Tags—Having trouble keeping track of club members? Make your own name badges using Kid Pix.

Pencil Holders—Use Kid Pix to make great-looking pencil holder labels for your mom or dad's office or desk at home.

Clubs and Teams

Have you got a secret club with your friends? Then how about some top secret club stuff to go with it? School club raising money? Have a raffle with Kid Pix tickets. Is your team competing in a race or game? Make number signs to attach to runners/players backs. Kid Pix does it all!

Membership Cards—Make secret I.D. cards for every club member. You can even draw a picture of each member on his or her card.

Awards and Ribbons—Has any club member done something outstanding? Give them an award or make a special ribbon. Kid Pix makes it easy to create.

Raffle Tickets—Is your club having a raffle to raise money? Use Kid Pix to design special tickets.

Runners Numbers—Design large number signs to pin to players backs in relays and games.

Delinquent Projects

For all you rotten, prankster kids, here are some goofy ideas for you to try. Remember, these are just for fun.

Fake I.D.s—Create your own identification cards using Kid Pix. Try making a driver's license or library card, or design your own credit card.

Note from Mom—Design a note from your mom to take to school and fool your friends.

Hokey Hall Pass—Use Kid Pix to make a silly hall pass. It just might get you out of class!

Too Cool Tatoos—Make interesting tatoos to stick onto your arms or hands. Or try putting one on your forehead for everyone to see.

> Dear _____,
>
>   Spike was very sick last night and unable to complete his homework assignment.
>   Please excuse him and don't give him an "F". Thank you.
>
>   Mrs. Spike

Gift Ideas

Having a tough time coming up with gift ideas? Let me help you out. Try some of these ideas for your next gift-giving need.

Baby Book—Design a special baby book for your new little sister, brother, cousin, or neighbor.

Gift Certificates—Create your own to give away to family and friends. How about things like: good for 1 free car wash, good for 2 babysitting nights, valid for 5 days of dishwashing.

Jar Toppers and Labels for Preserves—Help mom in the kitchen canning and making candy. Design some original labels for jars and tins using Kid Pix art.

Button Covers and Other Jewelry—Get really clever and fashion your own jewelry to give as gifts. Try making barrettes, pins, hair accessories, rings, watches, and more.

Make a Mug Cover—Use Kid Pix to create art for a mug or coffee cup. Dad or mom can take it to the office.

Covers for Houseplant Pots—Tired of plain old ordinary pots? Cover them with Kid Pix art.

Gift Tags—Once you've made a gift and wrapped it, use your computer to add a special gift tag.

Around the World with Kid Pix

Make a Flower Lei—Pretend you're in Hawaii and use Kid Pix to create an exotic flower necklace to wear to your next hula dance.

Crafty Kimono—Make a paper doll and a decorative kimono for an oriental flavor. This would make a great party favor or placemat decoration.

African Dance Masks—Design native masks that reflect the animals and culture of Africa.

Rainforest Napkin Rings—Design colorful, bright flora and fauna (flowers and plants) to make napkin rings for dinner guests. Parrots, jungle animals, and fish from the Amazon are also good napkin ring ideas.

Kangaroo Pouches—Make some nifty kangaroo-shaped paper pouches and folders to hold things. Decorate them with other Australian animal pictures, like the koala bear.

Punchy Pinata—Use Kid Pix to help you create a miniature Mexican pinata that you can stuff with paper or candy.

And What Else?

Create paper airplanes, door decorations, or bibs for your dolls. Design your own ruler, shopping lists, or paper aquarium. Make wall pennants for your room or to attach to your bike, miniature cars, a windsock, or sailboats. Decorate your lunch bags and computer diskette jackets. Make banners, bulletin board covers, license plates for your bike, bumper stickers, paper beads to make necklaces, or signs for the bathroom door (occupied, unoccupied). Create a tool belt with tools, lost & found posters, allowance reminder notes, and dashboards for your bike or the backseat of the car. Design thermos labels, scorecards for local games or action figure capes. How about shopping lists, a piggy bank, telephone "while-you-were-out" message pads, cookie cutter patterns, wheeled vehicles, or tooth fairy kits? Try making mazes, picture frames, paper stars to hang from your ceiling. Illustrate your poems, short stores, or make your own book. What about pop-up books? Design plans for building a clubhouse, or dollhouse, or secret invention. Use Kid Pix art to help you create crafts out of paper maché, clay, paints, and more. There's no end to Kid Pix creativity.

Hey! This Is the End!

Well, those are all the projects I'm going to show you for this book. I hope you had fun trying them all. The projects I showed you are just some of the radical things you can do using Kid Pix. But you've got to be a radical kind of kid to try them! Of course, you are—or you wouldn't be reading this.

There are zillions more great projects you can make using your Kid Pix program. Hey! If you think of any yourself, write me and tell me about them. Who knows—maybe I'll put you in my next book! There's always room for more Kid Pix experts.

In the meantime, stay cool.

Spike

Spike's address:

The Spike Man / Kid Pix Expert
c/o Alpha Books
11711 N. College Avenue
Carmel, IN 46032

Join the Alpha Kids Club Today!

The coolest computer users join the Alpha Kids club. When you become a member of Alpha Kids, you get a membership kit with an I.D. card. You also get:

- An 800 number to use if you need help with Kid Pix Creativity Kit.

- A subscription to *Kids Computer Forum*, the quarterly club newsletter.

- Alpha Kids disk labels, so you can keep track of your floppy disks.

- Other neat surprises!

And — here's the most excellent part — joining Alpha Kids is FREE!!! Just fill in and mail the card below.

Alpha Kids Club Membership

Print the required information on this reply form and mail it to:

Alpha Kids Club

a

alpha books

A Division of Prentice Hall Computer Publishing
11711 North College, Carmel, Indiana 46032 USA

Name: _____

Address: _____

City: _____ State: _____ ZIP: _____

Work phone: _____ Home: _____

____ Please enroll my child (children) in the Alpha Kids Club.

Name_____

_____Boy _____ Girl

Age _____Birthday _____

Name _____

_____Boy _____ Girl

Age _____Birthday _____

Note: Membership is free.